PRAISES FOR "PRECIOUS MEMORIES"

PEGGY POSTICH   PUBLIC RELATIONS SPECIALIST, CHILDREN'S HOSPITAL, OKLAHOMA CITY:

"The book is a testimony of how the human spirit rallies to cope and heal!"

THE TULSA WORLD:

"It's the heart working to release the pain it feels!"

15TH STREET NEWS, ROSE STATE COLLEGE:

"It's a really powerful book, you can't put it down once you start reading it!"

THE CLAREMORE PROGRESS:

"It's very exciting, apparently everybody likes it!!"

"The book is healing in nature. It's a collection of poems and prose directed at people who have suffered a loss!!"

THE DAILY OKLAHOMAN:

"A bright spot in the overwhelmingly sad aftermath of the April 19th terrorist bombing!!"

PRECIOUS MEMORIES

COPYRIGHT

1995, HEARTWORKS PUBLISHING CO.

All rights reserved. No part of this book may be reproduced in any form or by any means, electronic or mechanical, including photocopying and recording, or by any information storage and retrieval system, without permission in writing from the publisher. This is a compilation of material.

Heartworks Publishing Co.
P. O. Box 94386
Oklahoma City, OK 73143

ISBN: 0-9647602-1-5
2nd Printing

FOR
JUSTIN CORY COLE
AGE 7

THANKS FOR KEEPING YOUR LITTLE HANDS
BUSY STUFFING ENVELOPES,
FEET BUSY RUNNING ERRANDS
AND ARMS FILLED WITH HUGS

GRANDPA CHUCK
GRANDMA HELEN
MOM AND DAD (DEBORAH AND TOM)

FOR MY MOTHER, JANE D. DeMOSS

THANKS FOR YOUR ENCOURAGEMENT AND SUPPORT
OF THE IDEA FOR PRECIOUS MEMORIES,
AND MOST OF ALL FOR YOUR CONTRIBUTION
OF LOVE AND SPIRIT

DANIEL THOMAS DeMOSS

FOREWORD

When my loving daughter, Deborah Cole and her fiancee, Thomas DeMoss approached me with their idea of putting together a collection of prose and poetry in the wake of April 19th, 1995, I had mixed emotions as to whether or not I could do the editing even though I was a published author. I served in Vietnam and had experienced similar if not worse atrocities in that horrible war. I felt that the rekindling of those memories would bring them screaming to the surface to tear at my very being and I did not know whether or not I could deal with it. I had not gone to see the Federal Building for that very reason. However, out of deep love for my daughter and a sense of reluctance, I agreed to be the editor of PRECIOUS MEMORIES.

As material began arriving from every corner of the nation and I began to type the poems into my computer, I felt a deep depression begin to surface and the scars in my heart from Vietnam opened, and bled. I thought seriously about dropping the project and turning it over to someone else. I took a couple of days off from editing to recompose myself and to try and find a place deep within me for the horrors of Vietnam and the Alfred P. Murrah building to dwell until I could put PRECIOUS MEMORIES together.

When I returned to the computer, I selected a poem and began entering it. As I read the words, I realized this was words from the very heart of the individual who wrote it, words that told through expressions of love, caring and compassion, that AMERICANS TRULY CARE! They care about what happens to their fellow Americans, they care about the suffering, the grief, the turmoil. THEY TRULY CARE!!!

As more and more words began to appear on the screen, something inside me said I was doing this for a very important cause and that no matter what, I could and would, complete it!

With this renewed spirit that had been born in me, and with a new sense of peace, I eagerly read each poem or writing and with everyone, my peace grew deeper. I was now the vessel with which those who had expressed themselves in the pages of their writings could convey their feelings not only to America, but to the world!!

As you begin to read PRECIOUS MEMORIES you too, will begin to find that peace that only waits to surface after reading the heartfelt expressions contained in the pages of this book. Each and every word screams from the page and sounds its message of love for all to hear. All you have to do is read it to know what I mean.

May God bless all the little children and those who perished in the wake of the disaster. And may God also BLESS AMERICA, THE LAND OF THE FREE AND THE HOME OF THE BRAVE!!!

WITH LOVE

CHARLES E. (CHUCK) NORRIS
EDITOR

HEARTWORKS

This collection of Precious Memories is not about death, nor is it about suffering. It is about life, loving, caring and compassion. Most of all, it is about MEMORIES. Memories that will keep alive those who perished on April 19th, 1995. It will keep them alive because we want them to live. We want their memory to remain forever in our hearts and in our very souls, and by remembering them, they live through us. They are with us every day as we leave for work, visit a friend, read the newspaper. They are with us always because we have their loving memory.

Within the pages of this book, you will not find pictures or descriptions of the bombed out Federal Building, nor pictures of a baby in a fireman's arms. We have already seen those images and we have wept. They are forever burned into our memory, we do not need to weep over them anymore. You probably won't find professional editing, for I am not a professional editor. You may not find proper poetry format, for I have never edited poetry. I have never edited anything other than a newsletter. You will not find fancy paper or sparkling graphics, I could not afford it. But one thing I promise you will find and that is LOVE!! There is nothing but LOVE in this book and LOVE is all that matters. LOVE is more fancy and professional than anything man can produce. If you look closely enough, you may find my tears on the pages.

We are a nation of believers. We believe in our country and our fellow man. We believe the American way of life, though not perfect, is still the best to be found on the face of this earth. We believe there is spiritual life after death. We believe through our faith in God that we will find eternal Salvation in Heaven when we leave this life on earth as we know it. And we believe also, that those who go on before us have already found that Salvation. They have not died, they have only moved, to Heaven!!

The writings contained in Precious Memories are Heartworks. The heart of every one who has written their expressions of love, has opened and given itself to those in need of comfort and compassion. It is speaking to every one who calls Planet Earth, Home!! It has a message that must and will be heard the world over!! That message is one that cannot be denied, put aside or ignored. The message is a simple one; America will never be overcome as long as there is another American who is willing to go in place of those taken from us. And there are plenty who are willing to pick up the sword and continue the battle to overcome fear, oppression and terror!!! They are every where, they are our neighbors, our friends, they are US!! They are the rescue workers and fireman who risked their lives time and time again combing through the rubble hoping and praying they would find survivors. They are the policeman who put their lives on the line every time they don their uniforms to protect us. It is all of us working together to make America a better, safer place to raise our children and to continue our pursuit of life, liberty, and the American Way!!! And so, through us, those we have lost, will live. It is only when we forget to remember and love them, that they will die!!!
And if they die, America dies with them.

God Bless America!!!

Charles E. (Chuck) Norris
Editor

THANKS FOR A JOB WELL DONE!!!!

DEDICATED TO THE POLICE OFFICERS, FIREMAN, MEDICAL PERSONNEL, RESCUE WORKERS AND ALL THOSE WHO GAVE SO VERY MUCH OF THEMSELVES TO EASE THE SUFFERING OF OTHERS IN THEIR TIME OF NEED.

When the tragedy of April 19, 1995, unfolded, within minutes, the heroes and heroines of the day were immediately on the scene. With no regard for personal safety, they entered the ruins and began the recovery operation. Even before the smoke had cleared, their efforts were readily evidenced as they emerged from the crumbling and torn building carrying others to safety, only to return again for someone else. Around the clock, the effort went on in hopes of finding another who had survived the holocaust. Many hopes were dashed as time passed, but not the rescue worker's. They redoubled their efforts, took even more risks, spent more time in the building and undauntedly continued their efforts to find just one more survivor, just one more. Their efforts paid off, they found a young girl buried in the rubble and worked tirelessly to get her out. As they emerged with the young girls torn body, a cheer rose on the voices of those gathered there, a cheer that would be heard around the world as people sat glued to their TV"s, hoping, waiting and watching. Not content to find just one, they continued until all hope for survivors being found was over.

I saw many acts of heroism when I served in Vietnam. Many young soldiers, just common, ordinary, everyday people, who rose to the occasion when others lives would have been taken had they not risked or given their lives in order that others might live. I saw this happen many, many times in combat. And I saw it again in the wake of the disaster that struck our city. Just as in combat, I saw it many, many times. The workers may not have been facing bullets, bayonets, rockets or whatever other weaponry man had devised to destroy one another with, but they faced the same grave danger. They faced the danger of being buried in the rubble, should the wind suddenly blow, a pillar collapse, a floor settle, a slab of concrete come sliding down on top of them (evidenced by the death of a rescue worker when she was struck by falling concrete) or even another bomb detonate while they performed their humanitarian efforts. The dictionary defines hero as: A man celebrated for his strength and bold exploits. Heroine is defined as a female counterpart of a hero. This definition truly fits and is the only definition that could define the actions of those workers who risked their lives for others. I saw heroes 30 years ago, and I saw them again on April 19th, 1995 and the days that followed as they combed the wreckage and devastation for survivors. Many have said they were only doing their job and did not consider themselves heroes or heroines. A hero never thinks of his or herself as a hero, no, but others saw them as such as the events unfolded after the blast. Oklahoma City, Oklahoma, the United States and as a matter of fact, the whole world saw them as heroes. And in this country, Majority rules.

On behalf of myself and the staff of PRECIOUS MEMORIES, and all peoples of this earth, I say <u>"THANK YOU FOR WHAT YOU DID, THE RISKS YOU TOOK, AND THE EFFORTS YOU PUT FORTH TO ALLEVIATE THE SUFFERING OF OTHERS.</u> Words alone are not enough expression of reward. Your reward rests in the hands of our Master, Jesus Christ!!

CHARLES E. (CHUCK) NORRIS
EDITOR

ACKNOWLEDGMENTS

First I would like to thank the producers, my daughter, Deborah Elaine (Norris) Cole and her fiancee, Daniel Thomas DeMoss whose idea was the birth of Precious Memories. The amount of love and caring they put into making this a reality cannot be measured, it can only be acknowledged. And to my wife, Helen, for not griping at me when she came home from work to find the house stacked with poems everywhere. And a special thanks to her for mowing the grass for me so I could work on this without interruption. (We have 2 1/2 acres to mow!!)

I would like to give very specials thanks to the officers and members of Metropolitan Oklahoma City Chapter 568, Military Order of the Purple Heart of which I am the Adjutant, for providing the Color Guard for the ceremonies for the release of this book. And for their donation of the postage necessary to keep this project going and for their support and understanding as I put my duties as Adjutant aside and worked feverishly to meet our deadlines in getting this into print. Chapter 568 is the best group of American Patriots I have ever had the PRIVILEGE of being associated with!!!

Thanks to Tom McGraw owner of All-Star Screen Printing of Oklahoma City, for designing the beautiful cover of Precious Memories.

When handing out acknowledgments and thanks, there are two very special people who deserve more thanks than I know how to give. Mr. Jake Lowery, Director of Marketing and Public Relations, University Hospitals, and Peggy Postich of that same office: You have done so much, in such a short time. Thanks for sinking your teeth into this project and coordinating the publicity, and the use of the auditorium at Children's Hospital for the ceremonies for the release of this book. And most of all, thanks for the love and care that you give to our children through your work at the hospitals!!

My daughter said I should also receive thanks. But I choose not to laud myself. My reward will come when just one victim or one person finds comfort in the words of Precious Memories.

Last, but by no means, least, the biggest "Thank you", to those who sat down and poured out their hearts to comfort those victims and families of the tragedy of April 19, 1995. and then sent their Heartworks to me to publish. Without your expressions of Love and caring, this could not have been done!!!

Charles E. (Chuck) Norris
Editor

**IN MEMORY OF
LITTLE BAYLEE ALMON**

APRIL 18, 1994—APRIL 19, 1995

INNOCENCE LOST

Perhaps coincidence, perhaps not, Baylee Almon was born on my birthday. Maybe in the eyes of God this commonality was meant to be. Maybe God gave us the same birthday in order that she not be forgotten and God chose me to help insure her memory would live forever in the pages of Precious Memories. Whatever the reason might be, a great stirring from within drove me to produce this book of Precious Memories in order that the memory of not only Baylee Almon, but everyone who perished in that horrible bombing would be enshrined in these pages forever. Each year when I celebrate my birthday, there will be an extra candle on my cake in remembrance of them.

*DEBORAH ELAINE COLE
CO-PRODUCER*

POETRY CONTENTS

1—	THE VOICE OF THE CHILDREN	CHUCK NORRIS
3—	I SAW GOD TODAY	CHUCK NORRIS
6—	A MOTHER'S CRY	MARSHA KIGHT
7—	MESSAGE FROM HEAVEN	NITA EVANS
8—	DOWNTOWN	DEBORAH COLE & THOMAS DeMOSS
9—	MY MESSAGE	DELORIS CLARK
10—	TERROR IN THE HEARTLAND	THERESA LUCAS
11—	DARKEST HOUR, BRIGHTEST DAY	STEPHEN L. DeGUISTI
12—	THE RAINBOW PROMISE	LINDA ROSE DUNBAR
13—	UNCOMMON HERO	GARY J. KING
14—	THE HEARTLAND	KIM O'CONNOR
16—	TRANSISTION	RACHEL SMITH
17—	IN DARK DESPAIR	MERRIE KERSH
18—	O-K-L-A-H-O-M-A	GAYLA D. HIGGINS
19—	INNOCENCE LOST	KIMBERLY D. REEVES
20—	A NEW LITTLE ANGEL	SHARON E. ADAMS
22—	WORDS UNSPOKEN	JEANNEAN RADTKE
23—	TOGETHER AS ONE	AMANDA DOUGLAS
24—	A SONG FOR OKLAHOMA	JOHN PAUL FORSYTHE
27—	MORNING OF TERROR	ADREA M. HALL
28—	IN MEMORY OF BAYLEE ALMON	AMANDA FARMER
29—	TERROR IN THE HEARTLAND	MRS. GENE COCHRUN
30—	WHY?	STEPHANIE HARVELL
31—	WE MUST GO ON	DON BARNES
32—	CHILD IN THE SKY	MONICA BRINKLEY
33—	TIES OF THE HEART	Ms. DALE KEPHART
34—	TINY FOOTPRINTS	DAVID TIMMONS
35—	ANGELS IN THE HEARTLAND	TIFFANY WARREN
36—	WHERE WERE THE ANGELS?	BILL SHAFFER
38—	A CHILD'S WINGS	ANN HEIDLER
39—	THE DAY THE CHILDREN DIED	JOHNATHON ERIN DALE
40—	A LAND OF BROKEN HEARTS	CAROLYN E. SMITH
41—	SUNSHINE	JASON PITTENGER
42—	REMEMBERING YOU	ALTON CHARLES McCLOUD
43—	WEDNESDAY MOURNING AT 9:02	JOE SANDERS
44—	DON'T SHED A TEAR	JAMIE BATTAGLIA
45—	DOWN WHERE THE BODIES LAY	BILLY DEE HICKS
46—	TRAGEDY AND TRIUMPH	MARILYN GRIFFIN
48—	AND THEY SHALL KNOW NO FEAR	BRIAN CHILDERS
49—	AMERICA'S PRAYER	ROSE CHOTEAU
50—	WHERE IS THE LOVE	CHRISTOPHER SCOTT NICKEL

POETRY CONTENTS (Cont.)

52—TO YOU WHO HAVE LOST A CHILD................................LUCIELLE McGEE COLLINS
53—TERROR...AMY McDONALD
54—THE BUILDING ....BRANDON WAYNE FIELD
55—CHILDREN'S HOSPITAL..PEGGY POSTICH
56—MY BEAUTIFUL OKLAHOMA ....LAHOMA SMITH
57—A CITY CHANGED ....MARY MARGARET SMELTZER
58—RUBBLE AND RAGE ....DANNY FORT
60—GOD WAS WATCHING..BRENDA S. FEARS
63—REQUIEM..ELIZABETH HILL
64—GOD'S ANGELS ....JOLENE WILLIS
65—MY PRAYER FOR OKLAHOMA ....OMA NATION
66—THE MESSAGE OF THE BELLS..SUE CRAIN
67—I AM CHANGED..PAUL R. THOMAS
69—SHATTERED LIVES, MEMORIES AND HEARTS...........TAMMY LYNN PIERCE
71—THE CITY ....JUDY GILMORE
72—THE BOMB..TAMMY WHEETLEY
74—ALFRED P. MURRAH...DAVID RANDOLPH MILSTEN
75—OUT IN THE HEARTLAND ....LOUISE E. LARRABEE
77—TEARS IN HEAVEN...BILLIE KIRCHENBAUER
79—LOOK INSIDE..STACY MICHAELE COPENHAVER
80—AN OKLAHOMA THANK YOU..DANIEL THOMAS DeMOSS
81—A NEW DAY—A NEW FACE...BRINDA CALHOUN ROSS
82—WHY, LORD, WHY?...STACY PAYNE
83—THE VICTIMS..PHALA CLOUGH
85—TERROR...MARDELL K. (MUTT) POTTER
86—HEALING IN THE HEARTLAND...IMOGENE COCHRUN
87—THE BROKEN CASTLE...DARLENE ROGERS
88—THE HOPE OF THE CHILDREN ....MRS. FREDA LATTIMORE
89—THAT FINAL BLAST..MARIETTA PRITCHARD
90—I THINK I NEED TO PRAY ....MARILYN K. NICELY
91—AND THE ANGELS CRIED..BEVERLY SUMNER
92—A COLLECTION OF POETRY BY KATHRYN PERRY NORRIS
93—A PRECIOUS TREASURE...KATHRYN PERRY NORRIS
94—MY TASK...KATHRYN PERRY NORRIS
95—THAT'S WHAT AMERICA MEANS TO ME......................KATHRYN PERRY NORRIS
96—TELL ME NOW ....KATHRYN PERRY NORRIS
97—LET US WALK WITH JESUS...KATHRYN PERRY NORRIS
98—ALL GROWN UP...KATHRYN PERRY NORRIS
99—TO MY SON IN VIETNAM...KATHRYN PERRY NORRIS

POETRY CONTENTS (Cont.)

100—BABIES, OUR PRECIOUS TREASURE.............................. KATHRYN PERRY NORRIS
101—I SAID A PRAYER FOR YOU TODAY............................... ANONYMOUS
102—A MESSAGE OF LOVE .... MARIETTA PRITCHARD
103—TO UNDERSTAND WHY .... MARIETTA PRITCHARD
104—THE RIBBON... MARIETTA PRITCHARD
105—WE WILL NOT FORGET .... SARA MARTIN
106—THE BALD EAGLE MARCH... SUSAN SMELTZER
107—I KNOW YOU HEARD THE BUGLE CALL .... SUSAN SMELTZER
109—AMERICA REUNITED... STEVIE FARRAND
110—THE BATTLE ZONE .... PHIL BLACK
111—OKLAHOMA CITY TRAGEDY.. ROSETTA E. ROSS
112—TO MY CHILDREN.. JAMES C. YEAROUT
113—MEMORY OF THOSE WE LOVED .... NEALY STEPHNEY
114—MY BLANKET.. BETH ODLE
115—OKLAHOMA CITY, THE HEARTLAND .... SANDRA ROBINS
116—ANGELS OF OKLAHOMA... PAULA MARIE McISAAC
117—OUR FIREMEN .... KIMBERLY CHEW
118—A CHILD SPEAKS... ANNA SLAUGHTER
119—GOD'S WONDERFUL WORK .... CHUCK NORRIS
120—A COMMON BOND.. KELLIE SADLER
122—I CAN SEE HER NOW .... DONNA SAWATZKY
123—IN ANGEL'S ARMS... MARGARET MARTIN
124—A NATION'S PRAYER... AMY PARRISH
125—OKLAHOMA CITY 1995.. ROBERTA W. NORRIS
126—TO OUR HORROR... T.J. McCLOUD
127—FOR WHATEVER REASON.. DEBORAH ELAINE COLE

THE VOICE OF THE CHILDREN
BY

CHARLES E. (CHUCK) NORRIS
(EDITOR)

I am the voice of the children who perished on April 19th.
I am a little boy, a little girl, an infant baby.
I am no longer here with you because my life
Was taken suddenly, the reason I know not why.
I am not here with you in body, but never doubt I am present in spirit.
I am in the beautiful sun rise you see each morning
As you rise to greet each new day.
I am there in the furls of the Stars and Stripes
You lowered to half staff to honor my passing.
I fly on golden wings of butterflies, my beauty for you to behold
As I flit from flower to lovely flower.
I am the song on the voices of the beautiful birds who bring cheer to
Those who hear my song.
I am the gentle cooing of the Mourning Dove
As she tends her young in the treetops.
I am the cry of the Bald Eagle, the symbol
Of America, as he soars on lofty wings.
I am the breeze that blows through fields of amber waves of grain.
I am the gentle rain
That brings forth life on earth, my smile is the rainbow,
So beautiful to behold after the rain has stopped.
I am the ray of sunshine that finds its way
Through darkened sky. I am a tear in a rescuer's eye.
I am the memory Grandpa
Has of when I sat on his lap, and he laughed
When I tickled him. I am still the apple of
Grandma's eye. I am the love that Mom and Dad
Showed to me as I began my short life.
I am the laughter of my playmates as they
Now go on without me. I am the broken toy that
Dad fixed before I left this life.
I am the Teddy Bear that sits in its little
Chair, waiting for my return and the hugs I gave it
When I was there.

(Cont. on pg 2)

THE VOICE OF THE CHILDREN (Cont.)

I am the cry of the newborn as they first
Experience life. I am the babble as they learn to talk.
I am the shaky first step when they begin to walk.
I am the sparkle in the eye
Of a puppy, I am the fragrance of the
Red roses in your garden. I am the wispy clouds in
A beautiful blue sky.
If you will only see, I am there all around you,
And I will never leave if you will only look and see
Me through all these things I have told you I am.
I am all good things of this Earth and of life itself.
I am all the beauty you behold in life's panorama.
I am the love you have for me
That will never die. I am your memory of
Times past when I was there with you.
I am the picture on your wall.
I am the reason also,
That you must go on without me. You must
Cry your tears of anguish, you must put
Back together the shards of your broken life,
And you must go on.
And as you continue your life without me there is solace
To be gained from my passing as I now play in
Heaven with my Master, Jesus Christ.
I dwell in Alabaster cities whose streets
Are paved in shining gold, I lay down in
Green pastures on a bed of roses
prepared for me by the Angels
of Jesus, my dreams are only of my life
on Earth and the love you gave me while I was yours to love.
My playmates are the children who perished
With me and we are at Peace.
I want for nothing, no tears do I shed. I have only
Happiness and love all around me, I have nothing to fear for
I now walk with God. And when your time
On earth is over, and you travel to the
Great beyond, I will meet you in heaven and
I will still be, your child, for I will never grow old.

I SAW GOD TODAY

BY

CHARLES E. (CHUCK) NORRIS
EDITOR

As I was going to OKC
To see what I could do,
I saw God in a rainbow,
And he said:
"I need to speak to you!!"
"Me?" came my reply,
Startled at his command.
And then I noticed there
Were children all around,
He held them by their hand.
"Yes!! You" came His voice
Filled with pure sweet love.
"I need you to tell those left behind,
I have taken their precious children
To live in Heaven above!!"
I closed my eyes, and opened
Them again to see,
If perhaps my eyes were playing
Tricks on me.
But when I looked and saw again
That splendor in the sky,
I knew he had chosen me,
And I was not to question why!!
He spoke again and thunder rolled
As words came flowing forth:
"Take my message, Oh mortal one
To every corner of the earth.
Tell the multitudes that
I have come to see them through
What man has wrought on his own kind,
And I am sorrowed at the grief and
Suffering I find.
(Cont. on pg 4)

I SAW GOD TODAY (Cont.)

Tell them I have the little children
Here with me,
Their hurts to suffer naught,
To keep them safe, their lives
To live in pure sweet harmony.
The price was paid when their
Little lives were bought.
Tell the parents of
Those precious kids,
They are safe now from
All hurt and harm.
Their spirit dwells now
In God's uplifted arms.
And tell them too,
That in their suffering and grief,
I have also come to give
To those who believe in Me,
Precious, sweet relief.
To those whose child
I have taken this day:
I only gave him for awhile
For you to love, cherish
And watch over as he played.
To guide him, love him,
And teach him God's loving way.
Your job is done now,
You have accomplished much,
For in this child you have imbedded,
Love, caring and Godly trust.
Weep no more dear Mother,
Grieve no more dear Dad,
For Angels now have taken your
precious child to a place
Where there is no bad.

(cont. on pg. 5)

I SAW GOD TODAY (Cont.)

*Take comfort in my words,
Your trust in me you must place
And when I come again for you,
You will look upon
You child's bright, shining face.
And you will dwell forever
In my Heaven up above,
To reap the harvest
Of a child's precious,
Sweet undoubting Love."
The voice became silent,
As if it had never been.
Suddenly a bright, blinding light
Came from the rainbow within.
I turned my head,
The light I could not bare,
And when I looked again,
There was nothing there.
I turned to leave,
Wondering if this had really
Happened to me.
And as I opened the door
To the car to get back in,
I noticed at my feet laying there,
A brilliant rose,
Its color I had never seen.
I picked it up and as I did,
Its fragrance filled the air.
I looked up to Heaven
Towards the now bright sun,
And found my answer
Waiting there,
The Healing had begun!!*

**IN MEMORY OF MY BELOVED DAUGHTER
FRANKIE ANN MERRELL
OCTOBER 25, 1971-APRIL 19, 1995
AND IN HONOR OF THOSE THAT HELPED**

This very special, heart warming poem was sent in by a Mother who lost her beloved daughter in the bombing of the Federal Building on April 19, 1995. I am very touched by this writing. May God comfort you Mrs. Kight, in your time of sorrow. And may you find peace and understanding in the pages that follow as you read the messages of love contained herein.

*Chuck Norris
Editor*

A MOTHER'S CRY

BY

MARSHA ANN KIGHT

*Restless, restless is my heart,
Running fast, moving slow.
Sleepless in the night,
My mind wanders in restless flight.
Anger, fury, peace be still,
My heart rides her own free will.
Peaceful waters, are there none?
My heart cries: "What have we done?"
Wake up world, are we insane,
Endless price, this is no game.
Caring, sharing, it must be done.
Not for just a few
But for everyone.
Not just for today or a year or two.
A way of life, America I knew.
We must unite. we must be one,
Loss of life by man undone.
For a sacrifice this great,
Must wake us up,
Or be our fate!!
What a price to pay
For men that hate.
When I am old and gray,
I hope I can look back and say:
"Our children did not die in vain,
But united this country,
Once again!!!*

MESSAGE FROM HEAVEN

BY

NITA EVANS

Oh mommy, wipe your tears away,
There is no need to be sad.
They're taking real good care of me,
It's the most fun I've ever had.

You won't believe how pretty it is,
Yes it's really neat.
Why, this morning I got up early
And played near Jesus' feet.

Don't worry about that day anymore,
It was all so very sudden.
One second I was there,
The next, I was in Heaven.

There are many, many Angels here
To help in every way.
Jesus said he'll send you some for comfort
Throughout the day.

Oh, Mommy, I know you miss me
And long to hold me tight,
But I'm really very happy here,
I'm not even scared at night.

It won't be long until you come
To be here with me, too.
Believe me when I tell you Mom,
You'll never again be blue.

But till that day, remember
Jesus is watching you from above.
He's ready to take your hurt and sadness,
And fill you with his love.

DOWNTOWN

BY

*DEBORAH ELAINE COLE &
DANIEL THOMAS DeMOSS*

*We went downtown to see if it was true,
It was total chaos, like an Oklahoma City Zoo.
Portable pay phones, satellite dishes,
Reporters piled in, too many to list.
Horses and dogs,
Plenty of food,
Too many news reporters to elude.*

*Many people pushing and
shoving through the crowd,
trying to get to places
they were not allowed.
All of the officers on guard,
found that keeping people
back was very hard.*

*From sun-up to sun-down,
people still hung around.
Some wanted to help,
others just viewed.
We felt helpless,
there was nothing we could do.
We wanted to help others
begin to heal,
so we encouraged them
to write how they feel.
As the letters of love
began to pour in,
we have placed them on
these pages within.
We hope you find comfort
on the pages as you look,
because LOVE is the tie,
that binds this book!!*

MY MESSAGE

BY

DELORIS CLARK

I have a message for you today,
let me whisper it in your ear.
There is always a silver lining,
when storm clouds start to appear.

Although the path is rocky,
now on which we tread,
I am right behind you,
to claim your fear and dread.

The enemy came up against us,
and terror, his fury released.
Remember, I've been there before you,
I am the "Prince of Peace!!"

When you feel completely helpless,
there are things you can't understand,
I am the God of circumstances,
I'm guiding you, just hold my hand.

Though you are passing through sorrow,
burdened down with sickness and grief,
I am your God, your comforter,
in me you'll find, sweet, sweet relief.

Lo, I am with you always,
It's very true my friend,
I will guard you closely,
till you life on earth shall end.

Loved one, please just remember,
that you are not alone,
I'll be right there beside you.
till you reach your Heavenly home!!

TERROR IN THE HEARTLAND

BY

THERESA LUCAS

An early spring morning,
a strong building standing tall.
Yet in only seconds,
it was robbed of it's great strong walls.

Answering the cries for help,
tireless efforts were made.
A rescue worker gave her life,
but her memory will never fade.

Images of man's compassion
for his fellow man, voices across the nation,
remind us, we're in God's hands!!

In the midst of such sorrow,
it must be known,
our children are not hurting,
but are Angels,
now called back home.

Reminders all around the city,
headlights and yellow ribbons too,
flags flown at half staff,
and then there's the ribbons of blue.

Some one cries for the children,
as they think of the devastation and harm.
We cannot forget the picture
of the little girl in the fireman's arms.

The days go by,
the wind and the rain,
praying with the rescue workers
that some survivors still remain.

Terror in the Heartland
it has since been called,
though we will let no one
stop the healing,
only the building will fall.

DARKEST HOUR, BRIGHTEST DAY

BY

STEPHEN L. DeGUISTI

*In the heartland of America,
where a nation gets its soul,
an innocence was shattered
when evil claimed its toll.*

*With premeditated swiftness,
terror struck the plain,
and in its wake lay
devastation, misery and pain.*

*But the battle was not over,
and before the dust could clear,
good rose from the ashes
and fought back without fear.*

*Countless heroines and heroes
of every color, class and creed,
without pause came forth
and gave themselves to
all who suffered need.*

*The grace and compassion
shown us in this way,
have transformed our darkest hour
into our brightest day.*

*From the heartland to the mountain,
from sea to shining sea,
evil shall never vanquish
those who cherish Liberty!!*

THE RAINBOW PROMISE

BY

LINDA ROSE DUNBAR

FOR

MARSHA ROSE KIGHT

At 7:10 P.M. on Sunday night following "A Time To Heal" on the National Day Of Mourning, I pulled onto Interstate 40 heading East towards downtown Oklahoma City. At 1:30 P.M. that day, my cousin's daughter, Frankie Ann Merrell had just been identified as a casualty of the bombing. Her mother had never given up hope until her daughter was actually identified.

Feeling like my heart was as heavy as lead but had been wrapped up in bandages, I wondered how this young adult man, brainwashed by a radical fringe group of terrorists could have cut off these limbs of deeply rooted Oklahoma family trees. In our personal family, our great-grandfather, George Rose, homesteaded two miles east and two miles north of Yukon, Oklahoma. When our great-grandmother came down from Kentucky to meet him, she brought an Elm which she planted. It became the largest Elm tree in the state of Oklahoma for about 30 years and had been featured in the <u>Daily Oklahoman</u> and the <u>Yukon Review</u> many times. Our family tree and Oklahoma's family tree had been severely severed.

Suddenly, when I looked up, I saw half of a rainbow with six magnificent colors stretching halfway across downtown Oklahoma City. Then, as I drove on, it expanded to make a complete, unbelievable rainbow all across our heartland western sky. The beauty of this scene will be forever imprinted on my mind.

I wished so that all the families of the victims could have seen it, and as a matter of fact, that all Oklahoman's could witnessed this spectacular display. Several people called into the local TV stations about it later that night I heard.

Let's adopt the rainbow as our personal symbol to think when we see one: "We in Oklahoma have led the way to healing, overcoming hate and fear, with courage and strength sent down to us by a Rainbow Promise." Maybe we could sew a rainbow at the top of our Oklahoma flag so we can always remember our loved ones and our healing time.

UNCOMMON HERO

BY

GARY J. KING

Nine o'clock A.M.
A common man,
9:05 A.M.
A hero by fate's hand,
Emerges from walls crumbling and torn,
And races back in to save the newborn.

Denying the danger, Ignoring their pain,
They continue to offer their help to the maimed.

Extraordinary heroes, you've touched the world
As a tragedy of unspeakable horror unfurled.

You've proven to all who've taken a hand
In this drastic devastation of our land.

that love shall prevail and caring so deep,
Can eventually dry the tears that we weep.

And the hatred of men, their evil exposed;
Can never break the bond of the love you've disclosed.

As our hearts are torn by the bloodshed at hand,
You continue to prove the goodness in man.

We thank each one for your free-giving heart.
May your example provide a place for peace,
And Love, and Caring to start.

THE HEARTLAND

BY

KIM O'CONNOR

*God has reasons we don't know why
For doing what he does
On earth and in sky.*

*We've learned to come together as a city and share,
We've learned that in Oklahoma City,
Everyone cares.*

*The rescue teams are excellent,
Volunteers, staff and crew,
Police, Red Cross, and FBI
And everyone else, too.*

*The horror of the heartland
Will never be forgotten,
From Washington to L.A.,
Oklahoma City to Lawton.*

*The friends and family we've lost
Will be with us till the end.
In our hearts, minds and soul,
Thank God we have friends.*

*The sights of horror we see,
Makes our hearts break in two.
We'll never forget this day,
We don't know what to do.*

(Cont. on pg 15)

THE HEARTLAND (Cont.)

*We all feel the pain
Of everyone around
It's tough to see this happen,
Hopefully, everyone will be found.*

*Maybe God was running short
Of his Angels up above,
He needed these special people
To spread friendship, hope and love.*

*He chose these special people
To be with him this day,
They're safe in Heaven now,
Their heads, they rest and lay.*

*We ask God to help
And be with us this day,
We pray it will be all right,
And soon, go away.*

*Our prayer are being said,
And hopefully they'll come true.
Hopefully God is listening,
To what we say and do.*

TRANSITION

BY

RACHEL SMITH

(DEDICATED TO THE WAITING FAMILIES OF VICTIMS OF THE BOMB)

Walking through pain,
Mountains and mountains of searing pain,
The weight of the yet-unknown hangs heavy,
The hope of resolution hangs out of reach.

Blank eyes glance, then turn away,
Warm eyes look, then burn and dim.
Both, not seeing, momentarily defeat reality.
Time does not measure the moments,
Moments measure the span of unlived lives
And stripped relationships.

Disciplined heads with willing hearts,
Strain to attune with the fragility of despair.
A despair, cradled gently with strength and courage,
Needing time to negotiate the mountain.
Entombed in a surreal world,
Together, transition upward.

Editors note: Rachel Smith was one of the counselors who had the opportunity to serve the waiting families of victims of the bomb blast.

IN DARK DESPAIR

BY

MERRIE KERSH

How often when in dark despair, they seek a warm embrace,
A hand to guide them back through grief,
A heart to understand.

But all too rare is comfort found, all too rare, a face
To gaze upon and feel at peace,
For those who weep alone.

Their tears, fast flowing, blind their hearts to comfort which is theirs.
Their very tears, the balm itself,
Is hidden by their fears.

Until at last, exhausted, spent, blood driving through their veins,
The burning angry tears submit,
A quiet sobbing, reigns.

So like a gentle summer breeze the tears caress their cheeks
They're not forsaken, they can feel,
They have a "friend", who "sees."

He sees their "need, their grief, their pain", their misery, He sees.
Who?, only He could send the tears. the solace from within,
Our tears are from and must return to Gods eternal stream.
Forever flowing, liquid gold,
Toward a Sea Of Dreams.

So weep my Darlings. cry my Dears, it will be over soon.
The time is near-you'll dry your eyes,
and there you'll see, The Dawn.

Editors Note: Merrie Kersh is originally from England. She was recently granted American citizenship.

O-K-L-A-H-O-M-A

BY

GAYLA D. HIGGINS

Oklahoma
The wind that swept across our plain was cruel
For a moment in time.
Though a moment, embedded forever,
In our hearts and minds.

Take Courage
For the waving wheat waves more sweetly,
Sending a greeting with love,
Waving hello to those taken,
looking down now, from Above.

Oklahoma
Every night we will sit with our loved ones,
And sometimes, we will cry
For all those fallen, to whom we said, good-bye.

Keep The Faith
But now, when we see the hawk making circles
In the last rays of sun,
We will remember like the unbroken circle,
How we came together, as one.

Oklahoma
Every color, every creed, helping each other,
Hand in hand,
Knowing we belong, forever,
Dedicated to this land.

Draw Strength
We shall be stronger at our broken pieces,
Once they begin to mend.
We will believe in God,
Who is able to heal our hearts, again.

Oklahoma
Goodness will triumph over evil,
Though it will take some time.
We will be fine, Oklahoma,
We will be fine.

INNOCENCE LOST

BY

KIMBERLY D. REEVES

It's nine a.m. and all is calm.
Two minutes later, we hear the bomb.
It is so loud, it shakes the room.
It sounds like a sonic boom.

When we see the news,
our eyes fill with tears,
In our hearts
We have some fears.

All those people so innocent in there,
All the rescuers seem so near.
They look for survivors, Still they find none.
No one has been found alive
Not since day one.

People are dead, we can't explain why,
This whole things so sad,
A week has gone by.

The relief teams still looking
With all their might,
With hopes of finding
Someone else, tonight.

Everyone seems to be pulling together,
helping with donations, and whatever.
We're sorry it happened,
No one knows why,
we can only wonder,
And try not to cry.

We hear reports every hour
Of the day,
And as we listen
All we can do, is pray.

IN MEMORY OF LITTLE TOMMY HAY

A NEW LITTLE ANGEL

BY

SHARON E. ADAMS

I can't explain
how I feel inside,
Now that my precious little one died.
I don't want to believe that it's true,
But deep inside, God, I know
He's with you.

Why? Why did this happen to him?
My bundle of joy and cute little grin.
I had plans for him-to watch him grow,
So many things to him I would show.

His first little steps,
And missing front teeth,
His teenage years,
When he would give me grief.

His life was so short,
It doesn't seem fair,
But through it all,
Lord, I know you still care.

(Cont. on pg 21)

A NEW LITTLE ANGEL (Cont.)

*I know my Son is in
Heaven with you,
Happy with his body anew.*

*Each year I'll remember
What happened this date;
A new little Angel flew
Through your gate.*

*His name in the Lambs Book of Life
Was found,
Now he is home with you,
Safe and Sound.
Some day we will see him
In Heaven above,
Then we will gladly
Show him, Our Love!*

Editors Note: Sharon Adams wrote this prior to the bombing in memory of a child who died from Sudden Infant Death Syndrome.

WORDS UNSPOKEN
BY
JEANNEAN RADTKE

<u>O</u>h ye of no integrity,
Have altered my faith in humanity.
That there is good in all mankind,
And to this fact, could I be blind?

<u>K</u>indred spirits from a passing time,
Say all hurts heal with each new day,
But how do you heal a heart that's torn,
From losing your love on a Wednesday's morn?

<u>L</u>eaving words unsaid and shattered dreams,
A kiss not kissed, it's so unfair,
or so it seems.

<u>A</u> new day dawns, anger turns to compassion.
New hope to find at least, one more alive
So they can go home to their family,
survived.

<u>H</u>aving been through such a despicable act,
It might be awhile for their coming back.

<u>O</u>r maybe, their faith will be renewed.
Each day, a new beginning,
For they have seen the other side,
When life was almost ending.

<u>M</u>iracles can happen,
We've seen it everywhere,
People holding hands and crying in despair,
But never giving up
Their hope to find
One more miracle somewhere.

<u>A</u>merica can never be the same,
No place could ever be.
But one thing we're certain of,
They can't take away our Liberty.

Editors note: You will notice that the first letter of each break is underlined. It spells OKLAHOMA

-22-

TOGETHER AS ONE

BY

AMANDA DOUGLAS
(AGE 15)

I was sitting in the choir room
When I heard a loud "BOOM".
It was much like the thunder that one night shook my room.

I was not filled with fright
Because I didn't know what was going on.
Not many minutes passed when in walked my Mom.

I then knew what happened when she sat down to say
That the Federal Building had exploded
and help was on the way.

"How could someone do this?"
One of my friends said.
"Don't they know how many people could be dead?"

I'm proud to see Oklahoma come together as one;
Too bad it is not a time
When we all could have great fun.

It's time to make a statement for all the world to hear;
That America is a country
We used to live in without fear.

Throughout the hard knocks and all the tough blows,
Oklahomans stick together
Even when a hateful wind blows.

Amanda wrote this on Thursday April 20th the day after the bombing. Her Father is a fireman, and helped with the search and recovery attempts.

A SONG FOR OKLAHOMA

BY

JOHN PAUL FORSYTHE

Oh my what a morning in such a fine city,
The spring air so crisp,
The Sun shining so pretty.
We watched in disbelief at the act
That would follow,
It made us feel sickly, empty
And hollow.

Many of us wondered why Oklahoma City
Was the bearer,
Of this tragic event, the
Grief and the terror.
It choked us all up
And no one could swallow,
But we responded as an Example for others to follow.

We looked to the Heavens
And simply asked; "Why?"
He would let such things happen
Let so many die.
But sometimes in life
We are put to the test
Our city's broad shoulders,
Where this burden would rest.
God gave it to the people
Who could handle it best.

Others would soon come
From miles around
To help us pick up,
A building fell down.
They risked their own lives
And ignored all the dangers
To help dig out friends,
Our children, and total strangers.

(Cont. on pg 25)

A SONG FOR OKLAHOMA (Cont.)

*We all watched in horror as they
Dug out the toys,
Reminders of life in
Little girls and boys.
Headlights, ribbons and
Three O'clock bells,
All constant reminders
Of the stories they tell.*

*As if not enough, now the
Hard rain would come,
Most efforts would stop
Or just become numb.
But not in our city
Where the people kept trying,
For they knew that this
Rain was only, GOD crying.*

*The lines started forming
Through high winds and rain
To donate items that
Ease others pain.
And no one turned back
At the length of the line,
To help people suffering
Was well worth the time.*

*Not all of God's tears
Were shed for the dead,
For today God would cry
Tears of joy instead.
He cried cause he witnessed
That people still can not
Turn their backs on their
Own fellow man.*

(Cont. on pg 26)

A SONG FOR OKLAHOMA (Cont.)

*We will never forget all
The people that died.
The way we all hurt or
The way we all cried.
But at the end of it all,
There will be celebration,
Because we've shown
"Brotherhood" to the
rest of our nation.*

*From Detroit to Houston,
New York to LA,
People will remember
The events of this day.
And when they tell their
Grandchildren, You know
What they'll say:
"Oklahomans are great People,
And Oklahoma's, OK."*

> DEDICATED TO ALL THE PEOPLE WHO WERE
> TRAGICALLY AFFECTED BY THIS HORRENDOUS EVENT
> EVERYONE IS PRAYING FOR YOU

MORNING OF TERROR

BY ADREA M. HALL
(14 YEARS OLD)

The bomb went off, loved ones were lost,
Children were killed, and this was the cost.

Cowards were the culprits, they terrorized our town,
They blew up the building, and the structure came down.

The city pulled together, brave people helped out,
They risked their own lives, to help pull the victims out.

There was a Day Care in the building,
and innocent children were killed,
I seem to keep wondering how
someone could be so hatred filled.

Three-hundred were unaccounted for,
and almost as many
Casualties were found.
the day the Alfred P. Murrah Building
fell fatefully to the ground.

The remaining debris
was stacked two stories high,
From the nine story building in which
so many people have died.

We give our hearts to the deceased,
the answer we all demand,
And we pray for the survivors of
the bombing of the "Heartland."

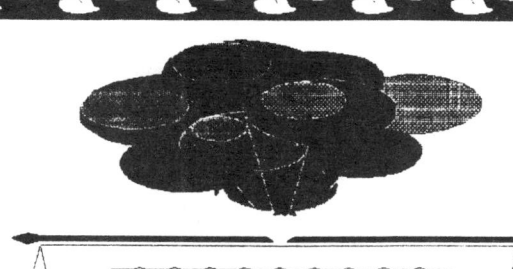

IN MEMORY OF BAYLEE ALMON

BY

AMANDA FARMER
(14 YEARS OLD)

Why has this happened,
What can we do?
It won't be the same,
Living without you.
I never expected this
To happen to me.
I won't be as happy,
Now watch and you'll see.

I left you at the Day Care,
Planning to take you home,
But when I came back,
You were unknown.
I cried, why did you have
To die, so soon.
Yesterday, we played
Your one year tune.
You were with me for
Only one year,
Watch my eyes,
They rain with tears.

TERROR IN THE HEARTLAND

BY

MRS. GENE COCHRUN

There was terror in the Heartland,
A bomb blast in a city so grand.
At 9:02 a.m., many people abound,
Nine stories came tumbling down.

Black smoke filled the sky,
No chance to say good-bye.
Twisted metal, concrete by the ton,
A cowardly act has been done.

Amidst the rubble and broken glass,
Hope grew dim as time did pass.
A lifeless baby held by a fireman,
Rescuers doing all they can.

Weariness comes from aching hearts,
Devastation and pain are only a part,
Then the tears begin to flow,
For still, no rest we know.

WHY?

BY

*STEPHANIE HARVELL
(12 YEARS OLD)*

*Why did it have to happen?
All the sorrow, all the pain,
People dying everywhere.
But, there was something to gain,
All communities have come together,
White, black, old and new,
So we could all help our family,
Together, me and you.*

*Why did it have to happen?
Those people weren't thinking straight.
A senseless act of murder,
Now hopes and dreams are sinking,
All of the world is feeling fear,
As we live, it brings a tear.
The heavens weep, we all cry,
Why did it have to happen, Why?*

WE MUST GO ON

BY

DON BARNES

So many things I don't understand,
Like the evil lurking inside of man.
We never knew, you and I, on that day,
The Lord would come to take you away.

Aware that only he knows the time and place,
I long once again to see your smiling face,
To touch your hand, to feel your love,
Are now all that I can think of.

And knowing you so well from the past,
I visualize your horror,
The moment of the blast.
No, you could not know that on that day,
The hand of God would take you away.

Nor did we know we'd not see you again,
We hope and pray you felt no pain.
Even though we watched day and night,
Hoping you would arise from that terrible sight.

Yes, our lives were changed on that day,
When the hand of God took you away.
Proof once again, only he knows
The time and place.
When, my love, once again we will
see your face,
In a land of love as we knew in the past,
With happiness we shared,
Before the blast.

We'll cherish precious memories till we
Meet on high,
While through the tears, our love
For you will never die.
And although we know your body is gone,
With a love never ending, we must go on.

CHILD IN THE SKY

BY

MONICA BRINKLEY
(AGE 19)

Dear Mommy and daddy,
I know I left you behind,
I wrote to tell you,
I'm doing just fine.

Although it hurt for a little while,
The Lord took my hand and said:
"Come My Child."

So now I'm here in Heaven,
With my friends who died with me.
While you are down on earth
Repeating: "Oh how can this be?"

I know you are scared, for I was too,
But now I'm in a better place,
Some day you'll be here too.
Until that day,
Please don't ask why.
And any time you see a cloud
Or a star in the sky,
Just remember, that's me and God
Saying:
"Please, please don't cry."

Love always,

Your Child In The Sky

TIES OF THE HEART

BY

MS. DALE LAWSON KEPHART

Our questions have no answers,
No one can explain,
No words or thought or actions,
Can really ease the pain,
Of the loss we all have suffered,
And the anguish that we feel,
At the loss of loved ones,
Our nations innocence revealed.

But Americans are united,
Linked in spirit and in love.
We'll rise above this tragedy,
With help from God above.
And we'll all stand together,
For in numbers there is strength,
To show that we're united,
We'll go to any length.

We'll look toward tomorrow,
With lessons learned from the past,
And seek to turn our sorrow,
Into actions that will last.
To insure that in the future,
We'll not be caught unaware.
Outrage will fuel our steady rise
From the dark depths of despair.

Let no one think he's able,
To tear our world apart,
For it is impossible to break
Ties of the Heart.

TINY FOOTPRINTS

BY

DAVID TIMMONS

*The Lord sometimes moves in
A mysterious way,
Suffer the children,
Or so they say.*

*Tiny footprints in the Valley
Of the Shadow of Death,
God will restore their lives,
With one mighty breath.*

*Now we must lay them down to sleep,
Our hearts will mourn,
Our eyes will weep.
Take comfort in the Lord,
For in his House, they now dwell.
He knows of our love for them,
And he loves them as well.*

*Tiny footprints now appear
On shiny streets made of gold,
As they now walk with God,
Their tiny hands he will hold.*

*Suffer the children, or so they say,
Take comfort in the Lord,
And we'll join them, someday.*

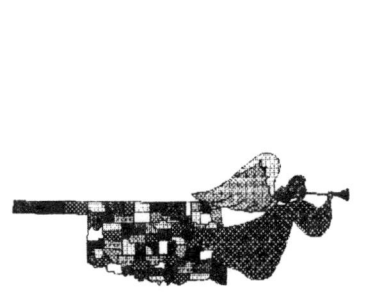

ANGELS IN THE HEARTLAND

BY

TIFFANY WARREN
(AGE 14)

On April 19, 1995
A terrible destruction did arrive.
The second floor with kids was filled,
Some still alive, but many were killed.
God said: "Come my children,
Take my hand. I'll lead
You to the Promised Land."

On wings of gold they answered his call,
They flew up to meet him,
With no fear at all.
He told them: "I give these halos
To you, with Love.
You'll be with me forever
In my Heaven up above."
They wear their halos proudly, you see,
Because Angels with God,
They will always be.

WHERE WERE THE ANGELS

BY

BILL SHAFFER

Oh what a beautiful morning, oh what a beautiful day.
On Wednesday the nineteenth of April it really did start off that way.

The children arrived at the day care, held gently in Mom's loving arms.
They were full of trust and expected us to keep them safe from all harm.

How could we know of the evil silently heading our way?
An evil that struck so swiftly that we were never allowed to say...

That your short little lives did have meaning as our hopes and dreams for you fade.
The hearts of all Oklahomans will be with you, wherever you are laid.

Your grandparents, your teachers your neighbors would give anything if they could say
A million things that were left unsaid in the wake of that terrible day.

We will always remember your faces. Your smiles give your kin such a pleasure.
Memories of your tiny embraces will fill their hearts like a treasure.

(Cont. on pg 37)

WHERE WERE THE ANGELS

(Cont.)

*As we think about all that has happened, evil things that have
caused us to pray,
we come to our God with the question... where were the Angels that day?*

*Where was their constant protection against things that come in the night?
Where was the love that was sent from above
And brought by those Angels in white?*

*Why do things like this happen? Children shouldn't have died on that date.
Beautiful children who laughed and played..
Now victims of people who hate.*

*The evil that hides in the forest should learn from these children of light.
With love for people around them, they were headed for futures so bright.
So we ask ourselves... where were the Angels? What were they doing that day?
What could God have been thinking as the blast took the children away.*

*There will always be times in our future when God's intentions are unclear.
Our faith should give us the message
That God still holds us so dear.*

*Our hearts are heavy with sadness and we really don't know why they're gone.
But our faith in your love and your wisdom
Will rise in our lives like the dawn.*

*The sun will come up in the morning and the birds will continue to sing.
The gentle breeze as it comes through the trees
The memories of children will bring.*

*Those children have gone on to heaven
where hate cannot touch them again.
They rest at the side of those angels
and our journey of healing can begin.*

**DEDICATED TO THE SWEET MEMORY OF THOSE PRECIOUS CHILDREN
LOST IN THE TRAGEDY OF OKLAHOMA ON APRIL 19, 1995,
FOR THEY WILL LIVE FOREVER IN OUR HEARTS AND
MEMORIES OF THEIR LOVED ONES.
BLESSED ARE THE CHILDREN,
FOR THEY ARE ALL
ANGELS OF GOD**

A CHILD'S WINGS

BY

ANN HEIDLER

We can find no rhyme or reason,
For there is no certain season,
When a loved one has gone away,
What is the healing word to say?

A gift from God is every Child,
To have known their smiles,
The light in their curious eyes.
Their laughter heard beneath blue skies.

This smallest Angel sent from above,
To have known a families love.
The touch of such a tiny hand,
Will help us somehow to understand.

So with wings they fly from our arms,
To play in fluffy white clouds,
To lose these precious gifts is hard,
Now they watch over us, and guard.

Who is to say when we meet again,
How comforting to know they are there
In our Lord's house, they will wait.
Until they walk through that Golden Gate.

THE DAY THE CHILDREN DIED

BY

JONATHAN ERIN DALE

The day the children died,
The skies opened wide,
And began to cry,
For the Angel's tears,
It could not hide.

The day the children died,
All of heaven cried,
And from the world,
It could not hide,
The tears of those,
Whose children died.

The day the children died,
The whole world cried,
For on that day,
Part of it, died.
And the painful memories,
would never subside,
The day the children died.

A LAND OF BROKEN HEARTS

BY

CAROLYN E. SMITH

A land of many broken hearts,
Our state has now become.
The tragedy caused by their "hate"
Has hit us everyone.

The devastation that was wrought,
The injuries, the lives that were lost.
The pain of every family touched.
It affected all of us so much.

The love poured in from out of state,
And touched our lives its true.
And now there's much we have to do.

For hate can be universal,
It can touch us everyone.
So we will all pull together
and pray: "God's" will, be done.

SUNSHINE

BY

JASON PITTENGER

No one you know walks inside,
Leaves a rose to make you cry,
A wall so high a place so dear,
A life so innocent, Can't shed a tear.

Can you feel the laughter
That you will never hear,
Can you chase away all that fear?
The sun still shines in heaven every day,
Saying; "Mother, I'll be OK, Mommy, It'll be OK.

The pain is deep, we wonder why,
So many people had to die.
We can see from our broken heart,
Our inner strength helps us survive.

Can you feel the laughter you will never hear,
Can you hold that life in your arms,
All in a flash, our lives, erased,
And all the walls came down.

Kindness flowed like water,
Kept our spirits high,
We can't replace
The sunshine in their face.
I'll remember till I die,
I'll remember when I die.

I find it so easy for a stranger to be,
The closest one to me.
An open heart,
I'll give to start,
For persons I clearly see,
But it won't replace,
The sunshine in their face,
I will see eternally.

REMEMBERING YOU

BY

ALTON CHARLES McCLOUD

Life is really hard to figure out,
There is always someone you'll have in doubt.
Don't try to figure out their mind,
It'll put yours in a terrible bind.
Sometimes these feelings are
Trying on my soul,
Sometimes I feel like
I'm one-hundred years old.
Not one day has passed
That I haven't thought of you,
Not one day; remembering
The things we used to do.
For I'll never find another
True friend as you,
To share in the good timesAs we would do.
So I'll sit and ponder my fate
From day to day,
But it seems like not one day,
Since my best friend passed away.
Father, please help us to understand one another,
So everyone will love their brother.
Help us show kindness with an open heart,
So a flow of sympathy and
Forgiveness can start.
Help us to be ourselves
And not an imitation,
So a cease will come to
This pathetic situation.
I want to know you and love
You in Every way,
I've waited too long,
And pray, today is the day.
If not today, maybe tomorrow..
But I'll sleep with a dream
Filled with sorrow.
And if this dream doesn't fade
Before I wake,
Please help me believe;
For my own sake.

WEDNESDAY MOURNING AT 9:02

*BY JOE SANDERS
(SIXTH GRADE STUDENT)*

*It was a beautiful morning at 8:55
It made everyone just glad to be alive.
A little boy was counting the bricks
On the Federal Building at 8:56.*

*Nobody had thoughts at 8:57
That so many of them
Would soon be in Heaven.*

*The workers all hurried at 8:58
To be at their desks so
Not to be late.*

*The children in day care at 8:59
Were being counted,
While standing in line.
The people who parked down the block,
Would get to their meeting at 9 O'clock.*

*A half-dozen people were on the run,
And got to the building at 9:01.
All was well, no one had a clue,
Of what was going to happen
At 9:02.*

*The blast, the rubble, no one could see,
The death, the panic, it was 9:03.*

*The building collapsed,
The living were crying,
Dismembered and crushed,
Others lay dying.
I'm told it happened by one
Terrorists hand,
As long as I live,
I will not understand.*

DON'T SHED A TEAR

BY

*JAMIE BATTAGLIA
(SIXTH GRADE STUDENT)*

*Don't shed a tear,
No matter what you do.
Yes, I understand she
Was close to you.*

*Don't shed a tear,
No matter what you do.
Even though you lost
Your dear child.
The person who did this,
Must be pretty wild.*

*Don't shed a tear,
No matter what you do.
Your child is in the best place.
Just remember the wonderful
Expression on its face.*

*Don't shed a tear,
No matter what you do,
Why did she have
To pay the price?
If only we could live twice.*

*Don't shed a tear,
No matter what you do.*

*Why she must die,
Only God knows why.*

DOWN WHERE THE BODIES LAY

BY

BILLY DEE HICKS

*The rain is coming down,
It's been steady all the day.
The search has slowed considerably
Down where the bodies lay.*

*It's four days after terrorism,
Down in OKC,
Rescue efforts have been halted,
There's no more life to see.*

*The evil that's in this world,
That's multiplied by hate,
Takes life from the innocent,
While mourners weep, and wait.*

*To understand the motive,
Someone's sick mind has planned,
To take the life from anyone,
How can we understand?*

*Reality has now set in,
By the evil in our state,
The day the devil set a bomb,
And sealed some Okies fate.*

*Just think about the families,
Who lost a child or two,
Or children losing parent,
What are they to do?*

*I know we all must die,
But I hope no more this way,
Time will heal our minds and hearts,
But we're still really mad, today.*

TRAGEDY AND TRIUMPH

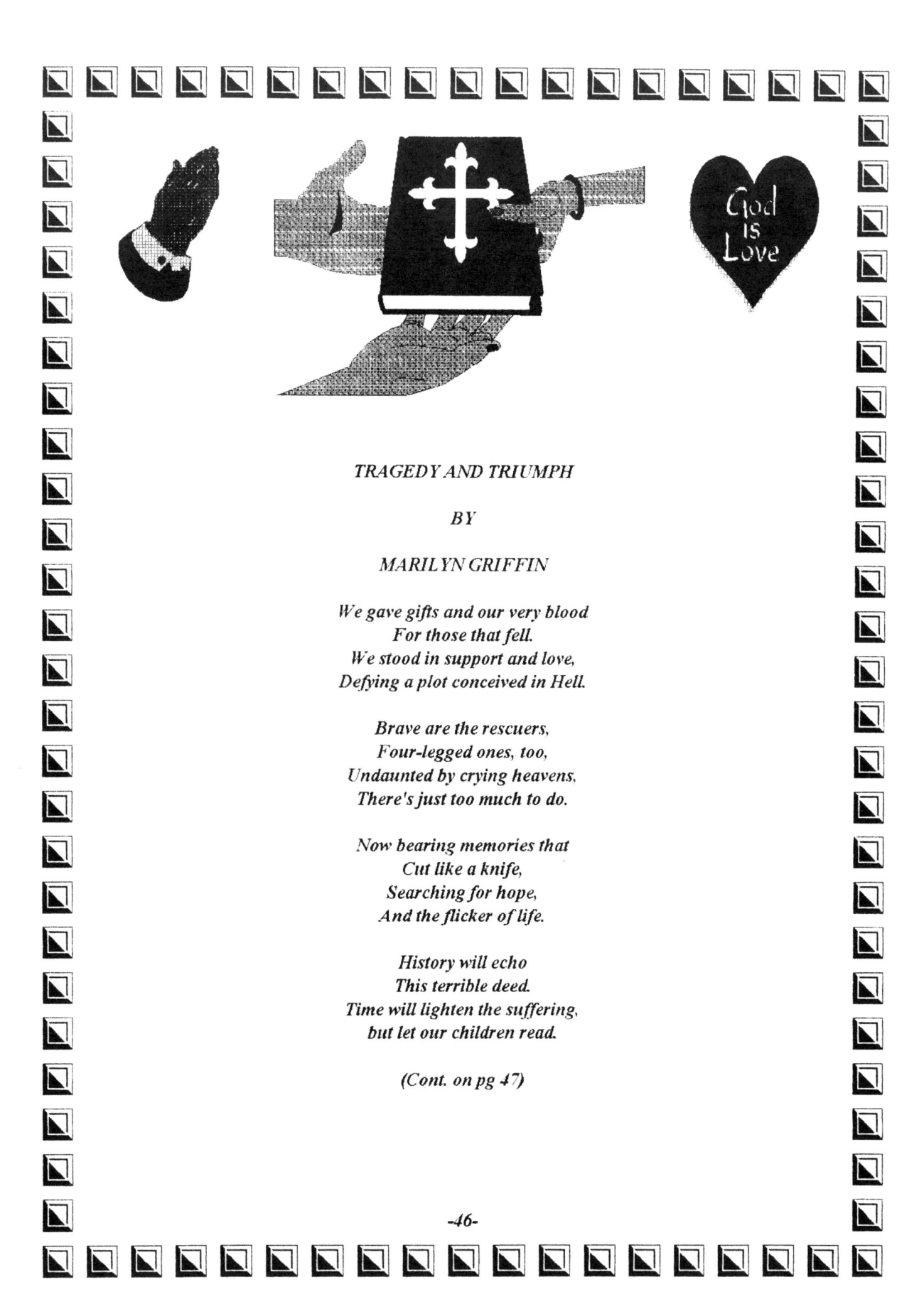

BY

MARILYN GRIFFIN

*We gave gifts and our very blood
For those that fell.
We stood in support and love,
Defying a plot conceived in Hell.*

*Brave are the rescuers,
Four-legged ones, too,
Undaunted by crying heavens,
There's just too much to do.*

*Now bearing memories that
Cut like a knife,
Searching for hope,
And the flicker of life.*

*History will echo
This terrible deed.
Time will lighten the suffering,
but let our children read.*

(Cont. on pg 47)

TRAGEDY AND TRIUMPH (Cont.)

*It was not anger and hate
Or despair that prevailed.
It was the love and
Brotherhood of a nation,
The wickedness failed.
Once again, God have mercy.
It is too much to stand.
How could one do this
To another man?*

*We stand and we wait,
Eyes brimming with tears,
We all need the answer,
To comfort our fears.*

*To each is a lesson,
For some, harder to bear.
But shoulder to shoulder,
This weight, we all share.*

*These words seem so shallow,
Nothing spoken will do.
The healing relief's not
In words, It's in spirit,
It's in you.*

AND THEY SHALL KNOW NO FEAR

BY

BRIAN CHILDERS

I looked into the heavens and sighed,
As the Angels bowed
Their heads and cried.
The light of their lives,
It flashed and died,
When God brought the children
Unto his side.

I called up to my God on High,
Is peace among men,
A terrible lie?
I prayed to my God
To tell me why,
When tragedy strikes,
Do our children die?

I look at those who
Have gathered here,
To say good-bye to those
We once held dear.
And down my cheek
Rolls a grieving tear,
For they go with God,
And they shall know, no fear.

AMERICA'S PRAYER

BY

ROSE CHOUTEAU

Heart in heart throughout this land,
Americans joined in prayer,
For the heartaches of
Our neighbors,
Pain that's felt everywhere.

Lord, heal the pain that
Racks our country,
As our hearts are filled with grief.
In a time of terrible sadness,
May his spirit bring relief.

Oklahoma City how we love you,
This whole world now feels your pain,
As we see the tattered building,
Longing to see it whole again.

Someday soon the pain will lessen,
Hearts will heal and bodies mend,
Remember that our prayers are with you,
This whole world is now your friend.

Heal this city now, Dear Father,
Ease the pain with
Your sweet love.
May each day now ease
The sorrow.
Give them peace from Heaven above.

WHERE IS THE LOVE?

BY

CHRISTOPHER SCOTT NICKEL

What melancholy moods,
Were scattered everywhere,
As tiny bits of glass,
Went flying through the air.
And all throughout the Heartland,
Good folks began to pray,
What happened to love, God?
Why has it gone away?

As evil fled the scene,
Mushroom clouds filled the sky,
Still no one could explain,
Why children had to die.
And all throughout the Heartland,
I heard confused folks say,
What happened to love, God?
Why has it gone away?

After floors pancaked down,
And smoke began to clear,
The town was put on hold,
A city filled with fear.
Yet all throughout the Heartland,
Thoughtful folks ran right away.
How can I lend my hands?
I'll help you every day.

(Cont. on pg 51)

WHERE IS THE LOVE? (Cont.)

Normal life put aside,
The town stuck together,
They had the nation's help,
But little gave the weather.
And now throughout the nation,
Newsmen began to ask,
When will the looting start?
Can they survive the blast?

Faced with sheer disaster,
Resilient from the bang,
No one took advantage,
Not even local gangs.
Now throughout the Heartland,
Grudge and hatred decreased,
Gangs helped pool up money,
To bury the deceased.

When we clear the rubble,
Memories won't leave our minds,
Still, we will trudge along,
Leaving travesty behind.
And all throughout the Heartland,
God's voice echoed everywhere;
"DEAR CHILDREN LOOK AROUND YOU,
MY LOVE IS IN THE AIR!!"

TO YOU WHO HAVE LOST A CHILD

BY

LUCIELLE McGEE COLLINS

You too have lost a child? Have no fear,
For though he cannot return to you,
Live your life that you may go to him,
When all your earthly duties here
Are through.

With these trials over, this journey past,
Why should we sorrow? Why should we grieve,
This is only a separation,
There is no death to
Those who believe.

That child's in the arms of his Father,
Calm as ripples that lap sandy shore,
Made whole by the pure living waters,
Clothed in love evermore, evermore.

Editors Note: Mrs. Collins wrote this in memory of her son who was killed in 1978. I felt it was very appropriate.

TERROR

BY

AMY McDONALD
(7TH GRADER)

Terror roams the streets at night,
Like a cat through a dark closet,
Destroying what it does not like,
Ruining what isn't it's own,
Taking away precious life,
Blackening our streets and lives,
As a shadow over the world,
It is unwanted,
Yet it comes.

It tries to tear the world apart,
Still bringing it closer together.
Terror leaves the smell of fear, of anger,
It brings tears and bitterness,
It tries to express it's feelings,
In a terrible, ugly way.
It is unwanted,
Yet it comes.

It makes the sky black with anger,
As the angry people.
It makes the sky cry with rain,
As the people's tears,
It makes the sun go away,
As our happiness goes
With the terror,
The puddles left by the rain,
As the blood shed of the victims,
The cold comes to make us shiver,
As does the terror,
It is unwanted,
Yet it comes.

THE BUILDING

BY

BRANDON WAYNE FIELD
(16 YEARS OLD)

The building lay in pieces,
All along the ground,
People frightened, scared, screaming,
Standing all around.
For terror has struck the Heartland,
The place that we call home,
Some people made it out with their lives,
And some are now, all alone.

No one can say what happened,
But we know why tears are shed,
We're crying for the ones we've lost,
The ones we love,
Those who are dead.

This thing that happened will change us,
From now till the end of our days.
And the thing that hurts worse are memories
Which will never pass away.

And you can't help but think,
What was it like in there?
Dead bodies, rubble, rock,
Broken window glass shattered,
Laying everywhere.

But now is the time to ask for help,
From the Lord our God above,
Now is the time to come as one,
And share our feelings of sadness,
Share our feelings of love.

CHILDREN'S HOSPITAL

BY

PEGGY POSTICH

*People called from everywhere,
They wanted to let us know, they cared.
We later asked: "Why do they call?"
It's about the children, one and all.*

*Pictures of children
That had been hurt very bad,
Were in all the newspapers,
Magazines and tabs.
All over the world.
People heard the awful tale,
And thousands took time out,
To send us so much mail.
Bears and bunnies came to us too,
To cheer up the children,
So they wouldn't be blue.*

*Hearts that were broken,
We thought would not mend,
Were healed with the Love,
That now has no end!!*

Editors note: Ms. Postich is a Public Relations Associate at the Children's Hospital of Oklahoma and saw first hand the suffering of our children

MY BEAUTIFUL OKLAHOMA

BY

LAHOMA SMITH

Scissortails on fence posts,
Rolling hills to climb,
setting Suns on Native ones..
Yes, once upon a time,

The Red Man set his eyes upon,
He liked what he did see,
And he would build and cultivate..
What it would come to be.

And men the color of rainbows,
Would come from miles around,
To touch the dirt and find the life..
The Red Man here had found.

Barefoot boys with fishin' poles,
Footballs in the air,
The gentle churn of oil wells,
Little pigs at county fairs.

Waterfalls in the midst of it all,
Red dirt thick as clay,
Sunburned skin and callused hands,
In the field to haul hay.

Where cowboys ride bareback,
On dust bowl legacies,
No storm of dust could change the minds,
Of those who wouldn't leave.

Was this a hundred years ago?
Or was it only yesterday,
Where wild horses and wild spirits
Ran free,
And no children ever died in the City.

A CITY CHANGED

BY

MARY MARGARET SMELTZER

The day had dawned so blue and clear,
Who could fathom disaster was so near?
Only those who planned it so,
As hours wore into early morn,
The devastating bomb, released,
Shattered and torn,
Took the building almost completely,
Down and away,
With precious lives, some injured,
Some with no escape, all day.

People turned to God to pray,
Help came from everywhere,
Everyone wanting to do what they may.
Great love for fellow man
Was shown that day,
And continued into weeks, without delay.

People were rescued, some injured, but alive;
Some not so fortunate,
Didn't survive.

It will linger always in our heart's memory,
That day that began so blue and clear,
We shall not lose faith,
For God is always near.
Only God can restore where there is
Suffering, pain and fear.

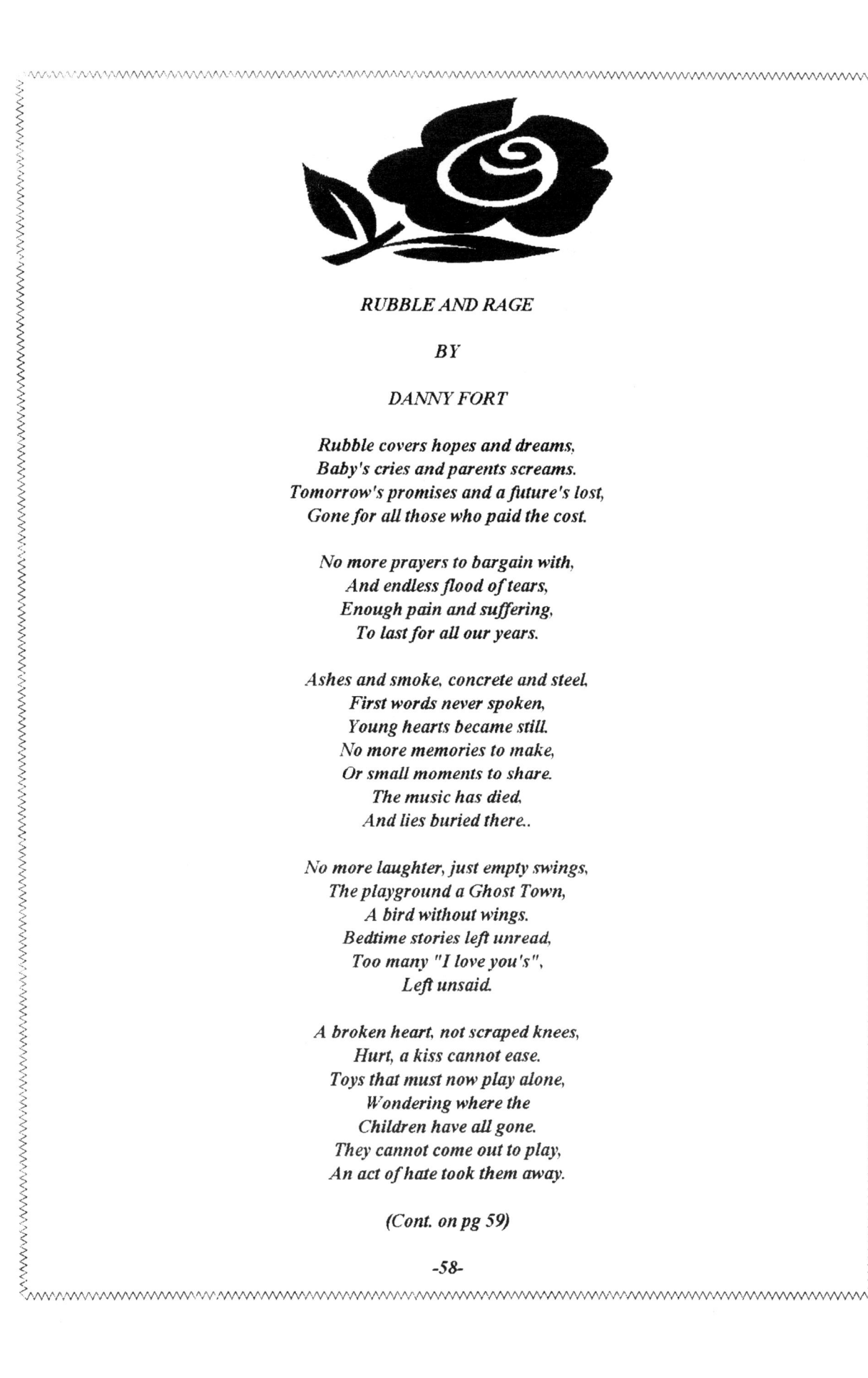

RUBBLE AND RAGE

BY

DANNY FORT

Rubble covers hopes and dreams,
Baby's cries and parents screams.
Tomorrow's promises and a future's lost,
Gone for all those who paid the cost.

No more prayers to bargain with,
And endless flood of tears,
Enough pain and suffering,
To last for all our years.

Ashes and smoke, concrete and steel,
First words never spoken,
Young hearts became still.
No more memories to make,
Or small moments to share.
The music has died,
And lies buried there..

No more laughter, just empty swings,
The playground a Ghost Town,
A bird without wings.
Bedtime stories left unread,
Too many "I love you's",
Left unsaid.

A broken heart, not scraped knees,
Hurt, a kiss cannot ease.
Toys that must now play alone,
Wondering where the
Children have all gone.
They cannot come out to play,
An act of hate took them away.

(Cont. on pg 59)

RUBBLE AND RAGE (Cont.)

*A night light could not
Keep them from harm,
The "bogeyman" has taken form,
And left us with
No one to trust.
For the monster dwells
Here with us.*

*And all the reasons
Make no sense,
When the victim is
That of innocence.
And I pray to God
They find rest,
And he will stop the pain,
Deep in my chest.*

*And heal the wounds,
And dry the tears,
And stop the hate,
And conquer fears.
And make the families
All aware,
That blessed are the children,
Now in his care.*

*A teddy bear that
Needs a hug,
waits in its crib like cage,
But all that's left,
Is grief, disbelief,
Much rubble and rage.*

GOD WAS WATCHING

BY

BRENDA S. FEARS

God was watching
The day Oklahoma City was bombed.
The day we lost our
Precious loved ones,
Little children, Dads and Moms.

As we watched our TV's in
Such shock and disbelief,
Our hearts filled with terror,
Pain and grief.
Upon the building we placed
Our flags and wreathes.

It seemed the world
Had just fallen apart,
Wondering what had happened,
And Lord; Where to start!!

Within seconds, as only He can,
God brought together
Both woman and man.
Fighting together,
To save, all they can.

Not thinking of themselves
Or the dangers ahead,
Only to reach the
Injured and dead.

In our darkest of hours,
When we know not
The Power,
The people of America,
Rose to the hour.

(Cont. on pg 61)

GOD WAS WATCHING (Cont.)

*To show that the world,
Still has in it, Love,
And God is still watching us,
From above.*

*We can't imagine how
Something so tragic
Could happen
Here at home.
This only happens,
In some faraway place,
Unknown.*

*As rescuers, fire fighters,
Doctors, nurses,
And hundreds of others,
Work desperately
As though they
Were brothers.*

*Millions of people
Filled the blood banks.
Just wanting to help,
Not expecting any "Thanks".*

*Just showing that the world
Still in it, is good,
No terrorist or killer,
Will ever, or could.
Destroy what's in our hearts.*

(Cont. on pg 62)

GOD WAS WATCHING (Cont.)

*America will stand together,
Through this and
We will, grow stronger.
Because of our love,
We will only last longer
Our prayers and support
Are all with the families
That have lost their
Precious loved ones.
We will not stop
Until Justice, is done.*

*God has taken your loved
Ones home to a
Beautiful place,
Where someday soon,
We will see them again,
Face to Face.*

*That glorious place where
We will never again be sad,
Or afraid,
Only love and laughter
Forever, because that's
The price, Jesus paid.*

"God is still watching us"

*May God bless America and comfort you in his Precious Arms,
Oklahoma City. We love you!!!*

REQUIEM

BY

ELIZABETH HILL

Last night I laid me down to sleep,
With troubled thoughts
Of bodies deep.
Beneath the bricks, the glass,
The stones.
Of tiny children's
Broken bones.

The silent shouts,
The soundless pain,
Like swollen bubbles
In the rain.
A picture grim,
In portrait frame,
Forever etched,
On mankind's brain.

Protect those souls, O God,
I pray,
Watch over those who've
Gone away.
Bless them with
Thy eternal light,
Hold them fast in thy Holy Sight.

On those who cry
For those We Love,
Send down thy blessings,
From Above.

GOD'S ANGELS
BY

JOLENE WILLIS

We are taught to accept,
And not question why,
But how could this happen?
Why did the innocent have to die?

Mothers, Fathers, Daughters and Sons,
Families torn apart,
Lives changed forever,
Only memories left in their hearts.

Watching the destruction,
Forever imprinted in our mind,
People wondering and praying,
They won't be alone
As they are left behind.

The precious faces
Of the children that died.
The heartbreak of their parents
Cannot be denied.

If they could have held them
Just one time more,
Hugged and kissed them
As they did the day before.

God must have needed more Angels,
To light up his sky,
And we have no right,
To ask him; "Why?"

Please take these children,
And make them
Little Stars,
And as we look up to Heaven,
We can send our love
From afar.

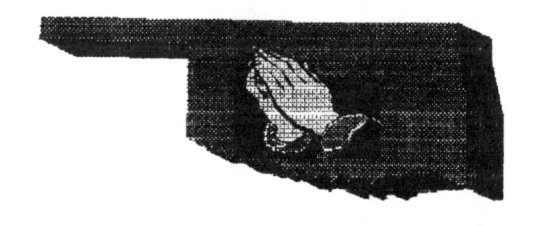

MY PRAYER FOR OKLAHOMA

BY

OMA NATION

As I lay down to go to sleep,
I say a silent prayer;
God comfort all the broken hearts
Of those who lost someone
So dear.

April 19, nineteen ninety five
At 9:02 A.M.
A chosen few were taken
I guess you needed them..
A Mother or Father,
Who was taken from the home,
And left behind the children,
Some, to make it on their own.

And for parents of an infant,
My heart breaks for them inside,
For the pain and loss they're feeling,
You know a part of them has died.

We know you have new Angels now,
Oklahoma is where they're from,
Take care of them,
<u>They're Special</u>,
They're missed and loved,
From this day on.

THE MESSAGE OF THE BELLS

BY

SUE CRAIN

Ring! Bells ring!
Ring for the babies that cry no longer.
Ring for the hearts
That pray to grow stronger.
Ring for the Mother's hearts,
For you know they are broken,
And for all the earnestness
Of the prayers being spoken.

Ring! Bells ring..across our land,
Help us know, We're still
In God's hands.
Ring out for freedom,
Ring out for truth,
Clearly a message for
Parents and youth.

Ring! Bells..pure and sweet!
Make us realize those
Babies are now at Jesus' Feet
Ring out for justice,
For whoever caused this pain,
The Good Book says you must forgive,
Again and again.

Ring! Bells ring,
A presidential command,
Bring peace and awareness
To our troubled land.

Ring! Bells ring!
And as your clappers peal,
Let us know Jesus loves us,
His love is so real!!

I AM CHANGED
(THE OKLAHOMA CITY BOMBING AFTERMATH)

BY

PAUL R. THOMAS

Your acts have changed a part of me,
I thought I was keeping safe.
I thought I was keeping
The children safe, too.
I was wrong.

My flinch response is now a short
Fused continuum
Of distractions.
Sudden sounds, peripheral
Flashes of movement.
Motive.

Yesterday, you were, perhaps,
A future acquaintance.
Today, all unfamiliars are
Future killers.

Yesterday, a hot dog cart
Being wheeled deliberately
To meet the sidewalk crowd,
Was just lunch.
Today, the cart may be the
Atomic instrument of
Someone's cracked righteousness.

At once, I want to know, why..
But knowing such things
Will not help me explain
Why the children are gone.

(Cont. on pg 68)

I AM CHANGED (Cont.)

*Your acts have changed
A part of me I thought
I was keeping safe.
The fearless child of my spirit
Must now hesitate
To trust.*

*Some say that this change
Is long overdue in
The Native Heartland.*

*The tear in my eye answers for me.
I am changed.*

Editors Note: Paul Thomas is an attorney who works for the Justice Department

SHATTERED LIVES, MEMORIES AND HEARTS

BY

TAMMY LYNN PIERCE

An explosion is heard,
Buildings shake from miles away,
Black smoke fills the air,
As glass shatters,
Stopping a heart from beating.

A young child cries,
A woman screams for someone to help her,
Panic fills the air and fills the heart
As people rush to the aid of the injured,
And the heart is stopped from beating.

A little child is lifted from the rubble by a warm,
Caring, loving Police officer,
She is then handed over to the loving arms of a
Firefighter.
But God has already taken little Baylee home,
Just one of the innocent souls
Taken home to Jesus.

Two young brothers, who lived in love together,
Are no longer in their loving Mother's arms.
Their innocence is gone, but their memory is there, forever.
Their is no pain or suffering for the boys now,
And their is no comfort for the parents grief.

Two other brothers are torn from their Mother's arms,
As God takes them Home to Jesus.
Tears are shed from every corner of America.
Even the sky cried and expressed its anger at this terror.
Who did this, why did they stop the Hearts from beating?

(Cont. on pg 70)

SHATTERED LIVES, MEMORIES AND HEARTS (Cont.)

God, please bless the kids, those who are with you now, and the injured as well.
They are the reason for our life,
They bring us laughter,
They bring us joy,
They give us hope for tomorrow, but for these kids,
There is no tomorrow.

Bless little Baylee, Danielle,
And Anthony, Bless little Tevin,
Dominique, and Zachary.
Bless little Elijah, Aaron, Kayla,
Chase and Colton.
Bless all the children whose
Souls are now in your care.
Help comfort those who mourn,
By restarting the beating heart.

Bless all the Mommies and Daddies,
Who lost their precious souls.
Bless the husbands who lost their wives,
The wives who lost their husbands,
The people who lost
Other family members and friends.

We may never understand,
But they will live their lives in your care now.
A radio plays, "Don't worry About the Children, Jesus has a
Rocking Chair."
It's hard not to worry and it's hard not to miss them.

But right now all these children are in Jesus' lap.
They don't need to understand,
They aren't hurting,
They don't know about the heart that stopped beating.

The heart that stopped beating is
the heart of America.
Oklahoma is the Heartland and someone has stopped its heart.
No wonder the whole world grieves,
Because the heart of our blessed country was stopped at
9:02 a.m. on
April 19, 1995.

THE CITY

BY

JUDY GILMORE

*The city grieves
For her children,
All too young to die.*

*Neighbors rush
To comfort and help,
To cover the gaping wound.*

*Prayers go up,
Survivors slowly
Begin the healing process.
Cleanup continues
In buildings and streets,
Hearts and minds.*

*Hope begins to dawn,
Slowly but surely,
Prayers spoken
Become answers seen.*

*The city continues,
Stronger and more
Caring than before,
Attacked, but now
Being healed and renewed.*

*Never the same,
New friends, new hope, new focus,
New love and respect for all.*

THE BOMB

BY

TAMMY WHEETLEY

*The bomb tore through the Murrah Building,
Ripping it apart.
The damage to the building was severe,
But nothing compared to the
Pain inflicted upon
Millions of hearts.*

*The death of so many innocent children,
Husbands and wives,
I thought there could be no good left
In a world that has destroyed
So many innocent lives.*

*But then I saw heroes of every shape,
Color and size.
Some were carrying out children,
Some were digging through
The rubble with tears in their eyes.*

*Some were carrying shovels,
Some were carrying medical supplies.
Their hearts were filled with compassion,
Their minds were filled with, "Whys?"*

*People came from all over the country,
Just to lend a hand.
The bomb hit Oklahoma City,
But it seemed to have shaken hearts
All across the land.*

(Cont. on pg 73)

THE BOMB (Cont.)

*I saw people giving so freely
Of themselves and
Donating so much time,
Wanting nothing but to help
The victims of this tragic crime.*

*We prayed for those still trapped,
To be rescued, for those
Who perished to reach a better place.
We prayed in silence that
The perpetrators of this
Terrible crime,
Would have a foreign face.*

*But our hearts were cut even deeper,
It chilled us to the bone,
To find out those terrorists
Weren't from foreign soil,
They were Americans, killing their own.*

ALFRED P. MURRAH

BY

DAVID RANDOLPH MILSTEN

Judge Alfred P. Murrah was a modest man,
Respected and admired in judicial acclaim,
He is remembered in spirit as we meditate
On the Federal Building which honored his name.

I knew him as a class-mate and colleague,
In the legal profession he was a patriarch,
The physical structure is now a memory,
The site should be re-dedicated for a park.

The dastardly deed echoed around the world,
Conceived in treason and nurtured in hate;
Oklahomans have proven their ability to
Cope with grief and the inevitable fate.

A park bearing the name of Alfred P. Murrah
Will become a symbol for generations to abide,
A garden of prayer for those who survived,
And a place of remembrance for those who died.

Editors note: David Milsten is a published poet, the Author of the official Will Rogers Poem of the State of Oklahoma.

OUT IN THE HEARTLAND

BY

LOUISE E. LARRABEE

*Out in the heartland in spring, Oklahomans
Had left off their children and started day's work.
In such a tall building..who could have expected
That outside, death-hands and disaster would lurk?
Yet silence was shattered and dreams and torn bodies
Were mangled and left in a steel tangled heap.
Bold crisis teams quickly responded to labor,
Sleepless, unrested, to help assuage grief.
Everywhere blood-bandaged people were staring,
Vacant eyes looking in stark disbelief.
"Where are the children?", this cry became anthem;
"Who stole their babyhood? Where is the thief?"*

*One rescuer held in his arms a small body,
Sobbing pervaded the crowds in the street.
Efforts redoubled to unearth the children...
Time was the essence that hampered their feat.
From the Heartland's far corners,
Saddened, moved nations came answer
To the trumpet call with hands and warm blood.
But death was the victor of one-sixty-seven...
Death from the cowardice of hatred and hood.*

*Why not at night when the building was empty?
Why not on Sunday when the churches were filled?
Though children were slaughtered, strong spirits abounded
Of love and devotion that will not be stilled.*

(Cont. on pg 76)

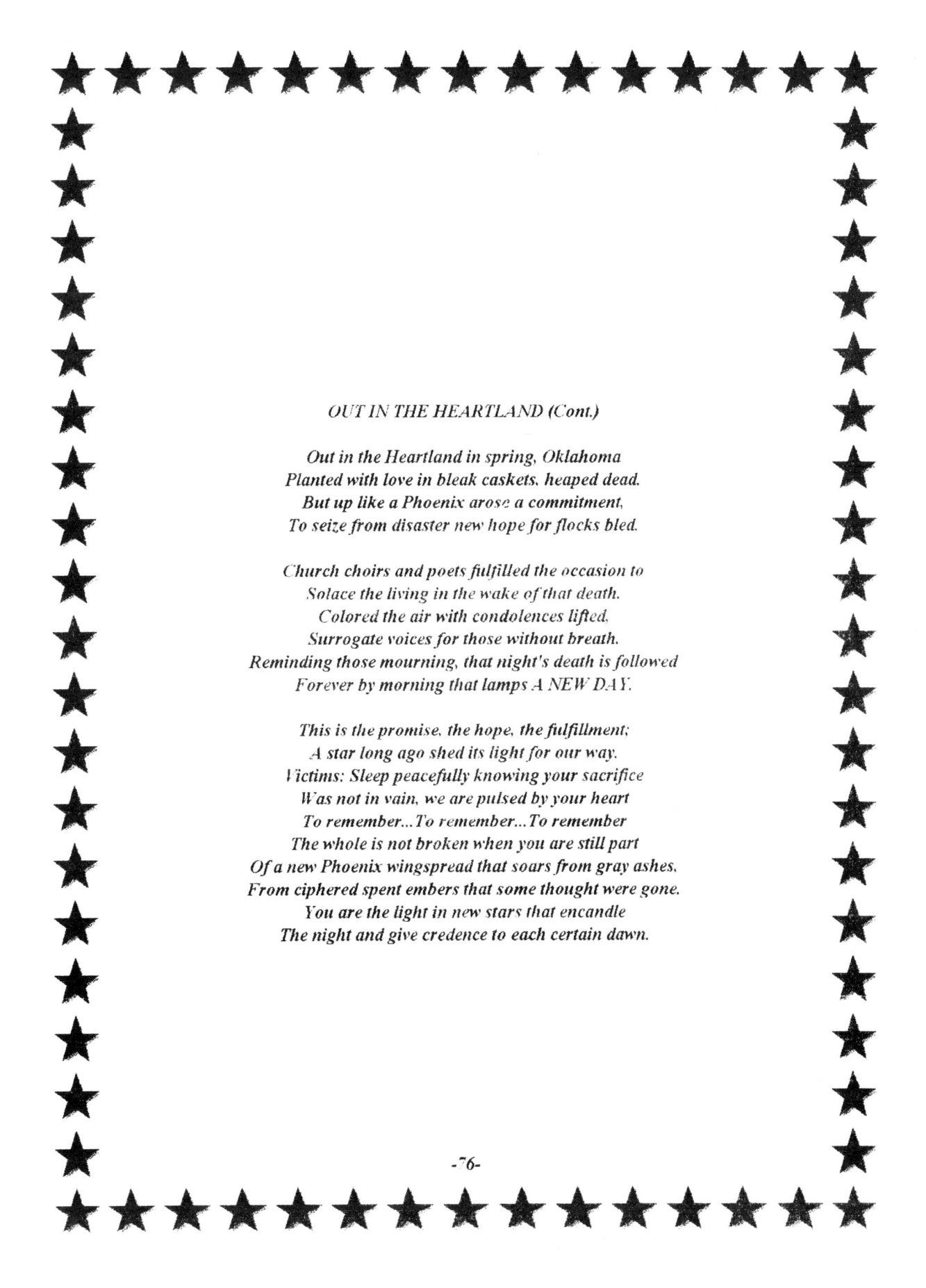

OUT IN THE HEARTLAND (Cont.)

Out in the Heartland in spring, Oklahoma
Planted with love in bleak caskets, heaped dead.
But up like a Phoenix arose a commitment,
To seize from disaster new hope for flocks bled.

Church choirs and poets fulfilled the occasion to
Solace the living in the wake of that death.
Colored the air with condolences lifted,
Surrogate voices for those without breath.
Reminding those mourning, that night's death is followed
Forever by morning that lamps A NEW DAY.

This is the promise, the hope, the fulfillment;
A star long ago shed its light for our way.
Victims: Sleep peacefully knowing your sacrifice
Was not in vain, we are pulsed by your heart
To remember...To remember...To remember
The whole is not broken when you are still part
Of a new Phoenix wingspread that soars from gray ashes,
From ciphered spent embers that some thought were gone.
You are the light in new stars that encandle
The night and give credence to each certain dawn.

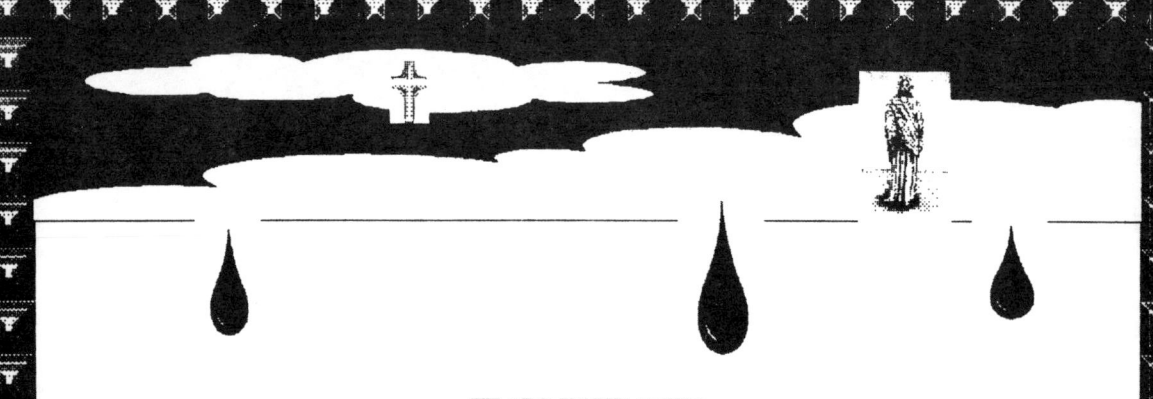

TEARS IN HEAVEN

BY

BILLIE KIRCHENBAUER

A community shattered by evil intruders,
As a workday began Wednesday morn..
A blast without warning resounded for miles..
And a building stood tattered and torn.

The workers were diligent as rescues were made,
Grim reality began to unfold..
As loved ones found and began to appear..
Many waited in fear to be told.

"How could this happen? Why can't we go in?
My baby is searching for me..
I left him just moments ago in their care..
Dear Lord, this just cannot be.."

But as hours turned to days, and our
Prayers turned to tears,
We hoped one more would survive..
As the rubble was lifted and pushed to and fro..
I heard; "Let my friend be alive."

With ribbons of blue close by every heart,
The arena serene with each speaker..
As the healing began with the words of each song,
The reality of rescue grew, weaker.

(Cont. on pg 78)

TEARS IN HEAVEN (Cont.)

*How uncertain is life as we know it,
We're here..In an instant we're gone.
There's no promise of even tomorrow,
For many, there will be no new dawn.*

*Our heartache and grief seems so heavy,
For those who have gone on before..
But the memories of good friends and loved ones,
Will be etched in our hearts, evermore.*

*If each of us lived as though this was "Our day,"
To give up our earthly treasure..
The example we'd be and the lives that we'd touch,
There'd be blessings of infinite measure.*

*A tree has been planted for each little one,
At the White House they'll see it each day..
As the Dogwood embraces each tiny new bloom,
They'll remember the children at play.*

*"Dear Lord, let us have learned from,
This sad, horrifying event..
We should ne'er let the sun go down on our wrath..
But each in his own heart, repent."*

LOOK INSIDE

BY

STACIE MICHEALE COPENHAVER

At 9:02 this morning I took my child's hand
In a moment of silence, I vowed to teach
Him anyway I can,
That white does not always represent good,
And black does not always represent evil.
We are all humans, we breathe,
We think and we feel.

We may look different because of
The color of our skin,
And the color and shape of our eyes,
But to truly see,
We must look with our hearts,
Past outside appearances,
To what's inside.

I think it very sad that only in a time of tragedy,
Is when people put aside their blindness
And truly see.

They open their hearts and they open their minds,
They come together to
Perform such deeds so kind.

This is nice,
But it makes me wonder when this time of need slowly fades,
Will the peace and this
New brotherhood of Man, stay?

AN OKLAHOMA THANKS

BY

DANIEL THOMAS DeMOSS

How do we Okies' really ever thank the heroes?
Yes, we may have even fed them Cheerios!
Maybe even a taco or two.
We couldn't have made it without you.
Our heroes without fail
continued to be right on cue.
When we Okies' need them most,
they never once left their post.
I think all will agree we had the very best,
they seldom even stopped to rest!
True, they are trained to acknowledge the worst,
it was evident their hearts' were about to burst.
Yes, we will never forget who they are,
we may never know how deeply their hearts are scarred.
As the weeks went on, let it be understood,
these Heroes did everything they could.
Never once could anyone say,
they had lost hope along the way.
Although over time we may forget their names,
our appreciation remains the same.
All of us Okies' thank you from the bottom of our hearts.
It is time for all to make a new start.
From all of us living in this great state,
We would like to set the record straight.
All of the men, women and dogs deserve three cheers,
no human should have to shed this many tears!!

A NEW DAY..A NEW FACE

BY

BRINDA CALHOUN ROSS

Today I take my steps a bit more slowly,
To notice the Earth of life around me.
Today I stopped for a moment,
My child to embrace,
And see the laughing eyes
And smiling face.

Today I squeezed tightly
My loving spouse,
And prayed the Lord watch
Over our house.

Today I marveled at the
Song of a bird,
Taking joy at the sound
Of each melodious word.

Today I woke with feelings
More intense,
With anticipation
Of life's events.

Today I awesomely seek
Each task,
To lend a helping hand
For those who pass.

Today I took a giant
Step in wisdom,
My face more set to
Preserve my freedom!

You may wonder who I am..
So with the voices of all
The loved ones we've lost,
We are the face of
Oklahoma City.

WHY, LORD, WHY?

BY

*STACY PAYNE
(AGE 13)*

*I don't know how to voice my angry feelings about this,
The bomb, the pain, the children.*

*It hasn't hit me yet, how sad this really is.
All I can think about now is how much I want revenge.
But, "Vengeance is mine", saith the Lord,
So I do nothing.*

*I ask the Lord constantly: "How could you let this happen?"
Yet I get no answer.
The question on my mind is simple: "Why?"
Yet when I ask it,
I get no reply.*

*I know the Lord has a reason for this,
But I can't imagine what it is.
What is the lesson we should learn
From a tragedy so terrible, so sad.*

*Is this the sign of the beginning of the end?
I feel he is coming soon, but I don't know when.*

*The questions we are all asking: "Who could do this?
How could the Lord let it happen?"
And the questions greatest on our minds:
"Why, Lord, Why?"*

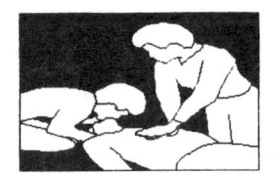

THE VICTIMS

BY

PHALA CLOUGH

I need your help and prayers.

I am there sifting through debris
Searching for life...and death.
Supporting crumbling walls,
Risking my own life to find others.
I am a victim too.

I am there containing the fire,
Helping to assist and lift rescue workers
Searching for life...and death.
I was the first on the scene
And the last to leave,
Risking my own life to help others,
I am a victim too.

I am there administering first aid,
Controlling the flow of blood,
Sewing the wounds, giving blood,
Caring for the critically injured,
Risking my own life to care for others,
I am a victim too.

I am there with my dog,
Walking through debris,
Searching for life...and death.
Risking our lives to find others,
We are victims too.

(Cont. on pg 84)

THE VICTIMS (Cont.)

I am a Mother, A Father,
My arms are empty,
My heart cries with loss.
I am a Mother, a Father,
My child was buried today.
I am a Mother, a Father,
Waiting to find my child,
Lost in the debris...missing.
I am a victim too.

I am the voice of the nation.
I am there to report the sorrow,
The loss...the destruction.
To relate the progress,
To describe the rescue efforts,
To keep a nation informed.
I am a victim too.

I am sworn to fight crime and evil.
I am there to sift through rubble
And destruction,
Looking for evidence,
Searching for clues.
I was one of the first on the scene
To help the injured.
Risking my life for others.
I am a victim too.

I need your help and prayers,
For I am a victim too.

TERROR

BY

MARDELL K. (MUTT) POTTER

A blinding flash, a thunderous roar,
Hell lurked there outside the door,
As shards of glass by blood washed red
Flew wildly round each helpless head.
By dust and smoke the scene was filled,
As walls crashed down on bodies stilled.
Terror walked within the ranks
Of living, stumbling, bleeding blanks
Whose eyes in anguish, looked ahead
Beyond the lines of living dead,
And searched the faces drifting by
For friend or child too young to die.
The eagle screams in OKC,
As feathers plucked there fall on me.
Truth will stand and surely find
Beyond horizons there to bind.
The faceless, mindless gutless few,
who, by their actions take from you
Your right to love, your right to see
Your Stars and Stripes Forever Free!!

HEALING IN THE HEARTLAND

BY

IMOGENE COCHRUN

Rescue efforts have come to an end,
Hope for more survivors grew dim;
Nineteen children were laid to rest,
A parents faith was put to the test.

We now pray for all the dead,
It's hard for us to just look ahead;
We've all read their names,
And suffered their pain.

For the victims we so grieve,
And the loved ones so bereaved,
But God's hand will lead you,
As each day you start anew.

At the Memorial service,
They did stand,
A single red rose in every hand;
A symbol of life and love,
As God looked down from above.

There were tears from the sky,
As their loved ones said good-bye,
The time for healing must start,
For time will mend a broken heart.

THE BROKEN CASTLE

BY

DARLENE ROGERS

The sadness is all around
Since the Castle came tumbling down.

Many children died that day
When they sat down, just to play.

For a moment we did not know
What shook our windows so.

But now we see it everyday
And wonder if it will ever, go away.

Many people were bleeding,
Crying for help
And desperately pleading.

Just like Humpty Dumpty's fall
Our hearts are broken from it all.

But, Mommy, wait, please don't forget
We are God's children without regret.

Please help me say a little prayer,
Give me a kiss and do not fear.

Jesus loves the little children of OKC,
They are precious in his sight,
Just like Me.

When the first photos of the Federal Building were shown in the newspapers, my three year old son thought it was a castle. I sensed his fear and sadness along with his four brothers and sisters and decided to write this poem through their eyes and hearts. We are only one family, I can scarcely imagine how the rest of Oklahoma and the nation feels about this human tragedy. Our poem is from the children who felt their home and schools shake and tremble on April 19, 1995.
With all our love.

The Rogers Family.

THE HOPE OF THE CHILDREN

BY

MRS. FREDA LATTIMORE

A bicycle here and a teddy bear there
And the death toll continues to rise.
A Fireman sits for a moment of rest
And wipes gritty tears from his eyes.

And the search rages on for John Doe #2
But he seems to have left not a trace.
Can there still be another in all of this world
With the hate of the first killer's face?

The argument grows about who is at fault
And the direction our country has taken.
But one thing is sure, there's no doubt at all
The peace of the Heartland's been shaken.

So where can we turn to escape desperate men
And regain the trust of our youth?
The answer of course.. we know that we can't,
We simply must look at the truth.

There's no peace to be found in the days just ahead,
Nor in all of the states of our land.
The only hope left for a peaceful heart
Is to remember, Our God has a plan.

There'll be no peace on Earth or in the hearts of most men
If we fail to remember THE STORY.
The last battle dies and there's no death at all
When our Lord returns in his glory.

THAT FINAL BLAST

BY

MARIETTA PRITCHARD

It came so quick that final blast, the black smoke filled the air.
"What happened?" I asked, but only silence lingered there.

I felt no pain, just disbelief and quickly started to leave.
I turned to walk away and saw God standing next to me.
"Can you dear Lord tell me why and explain this tragedy?"

"You're safe my child from all harm." replied our Lord
While he wiped away a tear falling from my eye.

"An evil person planted a bomb on the outside,
Hurting and killing both young and old,
The strong and innocent had no defense.

The grief's so great from what's been done,
A task awaits beyond repair.
Below mankind forms a single bond, mixed with sweat and tears.

The hearts flow with deep emotions inside,
Reaching out for love to comfort by.

Memories to mourn for many a year,
While others will treasure those to keep.

Scars will heal as time goes by, one day all life will be as one.
An eternal gift we'll see.

Pity the soul that's done this wrong, especially on Judgment Day!!
The time is near and yet to come, let's fall to our knees and pray."

I THINK I NEED TO PRAY

BY

MARILYN K. NICELY

*I think I need to pray,
grieving drains me of me,
leaving an empty shell with my name.*

*I think I need to pray,
because the pain is too great,
I am weak and I do not understand.*

*I think I need to pray,
to get permission
to see beauty once again.*

AND THE ANGELS CRIED

BY

BEVERLY SUMNER

Nothing gave any warning that morning,
there was no time, or place to hide..
A bomb brought all the walls and floors crashing down.
And In Heaven, all the Angels cried!!

Tears and sweat streaked the bloody faces,
as many hands reached to help those inside..
Bringing out injured people from everywhere.
And silently, the Angels cried!!

A tiny toddler drew much attention there,
while held in a fireman's arms, it died..
Stunned adults, broken and bleeding, stood back,
there, too, explain why, the Angels cried!!

Emergency crews swarmed over the scene,
casualties came on a blood-red tide,
their eyes reflecting their terror and fear.
You could see why, the Angels cried!!

Another child was carried out by a medic,
and from his grasp she had to be pried..
as he held on tight to her security,
Yes, even this Little Angel cried!!

While the world watched in shock disbelief,
in Oklahomans they all took pride..
and those days of rain was not rain you see,
it was really all the tears the Angels cried.

A COLLECTION OF POETRY

BY

KATHRYN PERRY NORRIS

On the following pages, I present the poems of my dearly beloved Mother who has gone to live with her master, Jesus Christ. It was her wish that maybe someday, her inspirational poems could help someone in need. I am granting her wish and I know that she smiles down from Heaven and her spirit will be present in the pages of her writings and her message of Love will be received by all those who read her words!

ABOUT THE POETESS

Kathryn Perry Norris was born Kathryn Perry, August 3, 1912 in Henderson, North Carolina. She passed from this life November 25, 1985 at Norman, Oklahoma.

Mother dedicated her life to Jesus Christ and was an inspiration to everyone. She taught a Sunday School class for over forty years. Her devotion to her faith in God and to her family was steadfast to the last breath she drew.

Kathryn derived deep satisfaction from writing inspirational poetry. Through the years she wrote more than one-hundred poems. It was her wish to share them with others, her way of giving inspiration.

At the time of her death, Kathryn shared a hospital room with a gentleman in a coma suffering from Parkinson's Disease. Doctors had given no hope for him ever regaining consciousness due to his condition. Every day she said a prayer for this man and comforted his wife when she came to visit. Several minutes before she closed her eyes for the last time, Kathryn said a final prayer for her friend in the bed next to her. Seconds after she was pronounced dead by her physician, the gentleman came out of the coma and recognized his wife. He said he thought he had seen an old woman walking by a lake of placid blue waters. This was witnessed by the wife of the roommate, Kathryn's grand-daughter, daughter-in-law, the physician, two nurses and the pastor of Kathyrn's church. The gentleman now resides at home with his wife and has improved considerably from his former condition. It remains scientifically and medically unexplained to this day!

Charles E. (Chuck) Norris
Editor

A PRECIOUS TREASURE

BY

KATHRYN PERRY NORRIS

*One little act of kindness,
one little word of cheer,
will help many a person
along life's road of fear.*

*One little word of praise,
a token of friendship and love,
seems like a blessing
sent from the One Above.*

*One little word of comfort
that will save another's soul,
is a far more Precious Treasure
than all of a nation's gold!*

MY TASK

BY

KATHRYN PERRY NORRIS

My task is to love someone
more dearly every day,
to help a wandering child find its way.
To ponder over a noble thought
instead of something
I might have bought.
To pray and smile
when evening falls,
and thank my Master
for my all.

To follow truth
like blind men seek the light.
To do my best
from dawn of day
till dark of night.
To keep my heart pure
for His holy sight.

When my task on earth is complete,
My Savior by and by I'll meet,
and I'll lay my homage
at his feet,
and live forever within Jasper walls
in the mansion he built for those
who answer, His call!

THAT'S WHAT AMERICA MEANS TO ME

BY

KATHRYN PERRY NORRIS

*Blue skies, rolling green hills,
fields of golden daffodils.
An old tree stump, a mountain high,
a babbling brook running by.
People working all day long,
in their heart's, one sweet song,
God help us keep our country free,
That's What America Means to Me!*

*Cities, large and small,
with buildings tall and white,
a flag-pole nearby, Ol' Glory in sight.
Ships that sail the shining seas,
children laughing as they play,
giving something in their own small way,
to help keep America free.
That's What America Means to Me!*

*The first Robin that comes in spring,
with the message of hope it brings,
the first violet to be seen.
Cattle grazing in pastures so green,
the smell of hay on a summer's morn,
fields of amber wheat and golden corn.
Stars that shine so bright at night,
showing the wonders of his might.
And knowing that this will always be,
That's What America Means to Me!*

*The right to worship as we please,
to the one who gave us all of these.
What privilege to live in a country so free,
God surely blessed this Land of Liberty.
That's What America Means to Me!*

TELL ME NOW

BY

KATHRYN PERRY NORRIS

If you have a kind word for me,
Tell Me Now,
for I cannot hear it when I'm dead.
Don't wait until I'm gone
to say nice things about me.
Tell Me Now, instead!

If there are any flowers,
give them to me now,
to enjoy while I'm living,
for when I'm gone,
there is no need for giving.

If you have any songs to sing,
sing them now so I may know
the joyous sound they bring.

If you have any praises,
don't wait until I'm dead,
Say Them Now, instead.

LET US WALK WITH JESUS

BY

KATHRYN PERRY NORRIS

*Are we walking with Jesus
every step of the way?
Do we tell of the love and comfort
he gives to us each day?
Are we setting good examples
for someone we hold dear?
Let Us Walk With Jesus,
having nothing in life to fear.*

*Are we living each day
as we know best?
Do we complain when he
puts us to the test?
Do we ever stop and thank him
for the hardships
he's helped us through?
Let Us Walk With Jesus,
he will guide us,
both me and you.*

ALL GROWN UP

BY

KATHRYN PERRY NORRIS

*It seems like only yesterday
you were playing grown up in my faded blue dress.
I remember, I had it packed away
in my old Cedar chest.
What memories came back
as I saw you standing there,
with mirror in hand,
combing your golden hair.
You borrowed my high heels, and my stockings, too.
My lipstick was all over your pretty face.
It took more than soap, it took cold cream
to remove that goo.
How I tried to get you to always
put your toys in the right place.
And when you wrote: "I Love You, Mommie",
It wasn't in the right place at all.
You wrote it on the kitchen wall!
It seems like only yesterday,
I took your hand in mine and
we walked out the gate
and down the lane to school.
It was your first day and you didn't want to be late.
It just isn't possible,
I've already seen you graduate.
Why it was only yesterday
I scolded you for teasing the pup,
But I realize at last,
the years have gone by fast
and my precious little girl is
All Grown Up!!*

TO MY SON IN VIETNAM

BY

KATHRYN PERRY NORRIS

*Our precious Savior gave you to me,
to love and cherish for all eternity.
I gave you life and watched you grow
into the finest of young men.
I was so proud of you back then.
Then one day you came to me,
said you'd been called to fight
for Liberty in a foreign land
in a far away place called, Vietnam.
Dad and I watched with heavy heart and dampened eye
as you boarded your plane and waved good-bye.
When those mighty engines roared, lifting you from earth,
I remembered the joyous occasion of your birth.
Then I asked my Master to see you through
and give you courage and strength for things you now must do.
Son, I know you are in the thick of battle being in the Infantry,
and I pray to God each night to bring you safely home to me.
But if the price of freedom must be paid with your life,
and God sees fit to take you from Dad, I and your loving wife,
Then I know he will take you to live on high,
to experience the splendor of his mansion in the sky.
When the war is over and battlefields are naught,
and you come back home to us from the war you have fought,
I will look on you with pride for the things you have done,
and I'll lift my arms to Heaven and thank my Gracious Lord
for giving me back my son!!*

Editors note: I received this poem from my Mother the day I had been severely wounded and lay near death in a field hospital in Vietnam. I think it was one of the reasons I am here today!

Written April 3, 1931

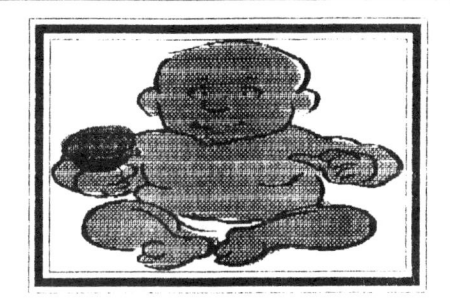

BABIES, OUR PRECIOUS TREASURES

BY

KATHRYN PERRY NORRIS

Babies are such Precious Treasures,
God loans them to us for awhile.
We care for them and love them so,
and cherish each little smile.
We wonder at all the things they learn,
and listen for the first words they speak.
We kiss each chubby little hand
and each little dimpled cheek.
They are the nearest things to angels on earth,
remember, the greatest gift to the world
was Baby Jesus' birth.
Babies are far more Precious Treasures than rubies or pearls
there's no way of measuring how much they mean to us.
They've no way of knowing the
happiness and joy they bring.
We make so many plans for them and the future
when they grow up as a woman or a man.
Sometimes we forget that God grows lonely
and He also has a plan,
and he calls these Precious Treasures above.
There is nothing purer than a baby's love.
Babies are more precious than the fragrant rose with the dew drops on it,
they are sweeter than the greatest Sonnet.
They are more precious than silver or gold.
The love and happiness they bring,
the heart isn't large enough to hold.
Although we are sad when with them we have to part,
we know that God understands the sadness in our heart.
We know that it is our love for a baby
that brought us love in full measure.
Yes, Babies are such a Precious Treasure.

I SAID A PRAYER FOR YOU TODAY

ANONYMOUS

*I said a prayer for you today,
and know God must have heard,
I felt the answer in my heart,
Although he spoke no word!!*

*I didn't ask for wealth or fame,
(I knew you wouldn't mind)
I asked him to send treasures
of a far more lasting kind!!*

*I asked him to be near you,
at the start of each new day,
to grant you health and blessings,
and friends to share your way!!*

*I asked for happiness for you,
in all things great and small,
but it was for His loving care,
I prayed for most of all!!*

A MESSAGE OF LOVE

BY

MARIETTA PRITCHARD

To endure peace, we must have happiness within.
Love will then conquer the world.
Freedom will spread its wings
like the purity of the White Dove in flight,
thus casting a shadow. covering the world
with the everlasting light of eternity!
The Heaven above will open with the
hand of God reaching out to each soul,
destroying evil and casting out all sins!

The wonderful feeling deep within,
the sharing and caring of our
loved ones and friends.
This is the gift of life to mankind,
the beginning of harmony toward peace,
beauty and love forever.
Sharing this message of love and rejoice
to fill the mind and heart
of each lost soul,
paradise awaits when
only in God, we believe!

TO UNDERSTAND WHY

BY

MARIETTA PRITCHARD

"I think I will, I think I won't
I think I do, I think I don't."
My mind's a mess and I try to pray,
"Oh God please make this go away!"
This torment of sorrow I feel inside,
why can't things be like they were yesterday?
So precious the past
I thought would last,
and what now remains is memories.

I reach out to hold or hear
a child's laughter with a
smile that made me smile back
with happiness.
A love reflecting from
the beauty in their eyes,
showing how much they cared.

One day, we'll be together again
and our long awaiting
journey will end.
This special poem has a hug and kiss
sealed inside to be delivered
by the Angels in Heaven above!!

P.S.

I send you all my love!!

THE RIBBON

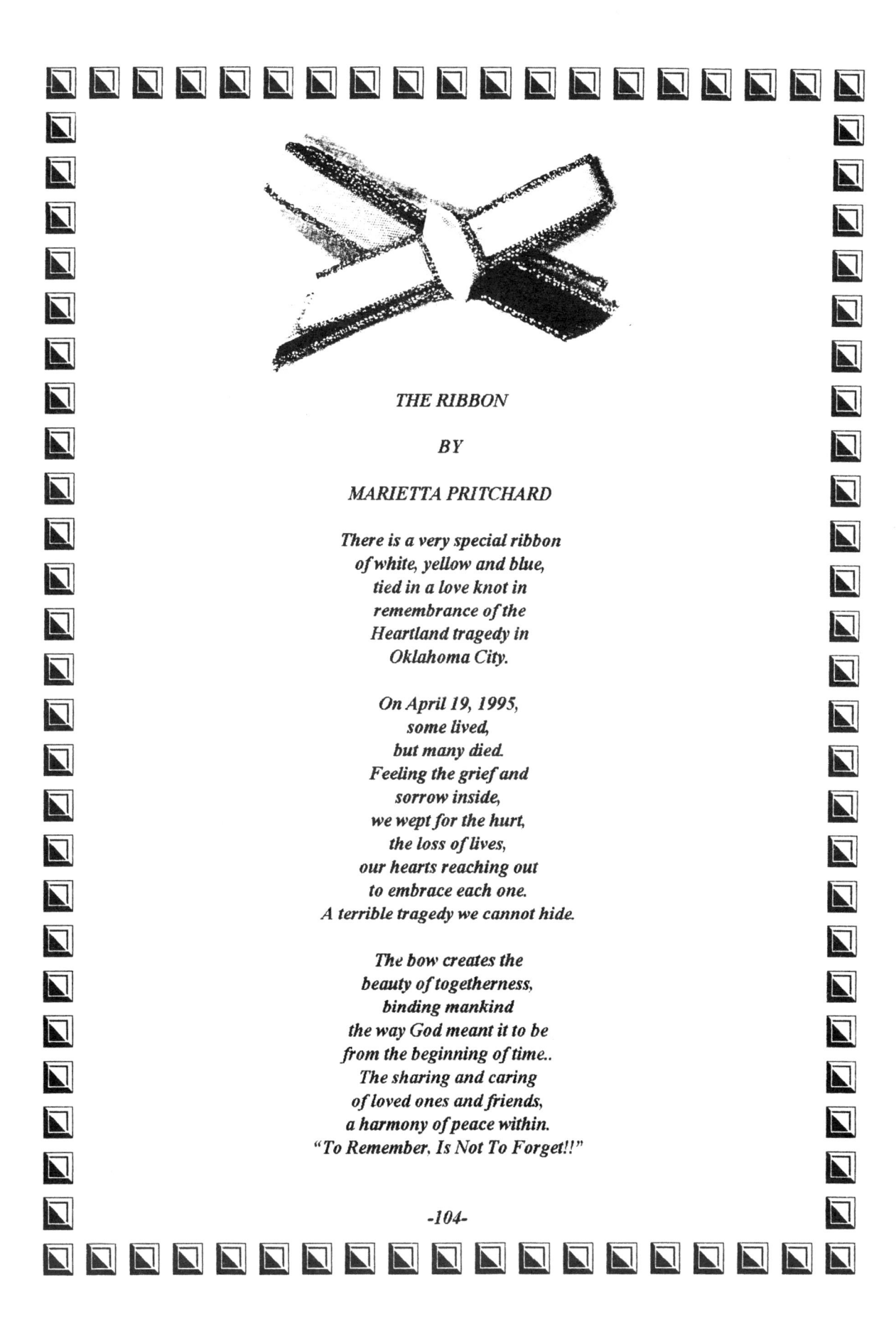

BY

MARIETTA PRITCHARD

*There is a very special ribbon
of white, yellow and blue,
tied in a love knot in
remembrance of the
Heartland tragedy in
Oklahoma City.*

*On April 19, 1995,
some lived,
but many died.
Feeling the grief and
sorrow inside,
we wept for the hurt,
the loss of lives,
our hearts reaching out
to embrace each one.
A terrible tragedy we cannot hide.*

*The bow creates the
beauty of togetherness,
binding mankind
the way God meant it to be
from the beginning of time..
The sharing and caring
of loved ones and friends,
a harmony of peace within.
"To Remember, Is Not To Forget!!"*

Living Memorial—Tree Dedication of Two White Bud Trees. The University of Oklahoma Hospitals, Oklahoma City, Wednesday May 3, 1995

Sara Martin wrote and presented this writing at the dedication of the two White Bud trees. Sara works for the University Hospitals

WE WILL NOT FORGET

BY

SARA MARTIN

"We will not forget April 19, 1995. We will not forget the shock that something so terrible could happen in our community. We will not forget the horror of death and destruction played out right before our eyes. Children with chattering teeth afraid to let go—the desperate voices of parents asking, "Have you seen a little boy brought in? He had on a red shirt and brown pants. They said he might be here. Have you seen him?" We will not forget the feeling of despair looking at empty gurneys and wheel-chairs, knowing there should be more patients...and then slowly realizing that there were no more survivors. We will not forget April 19, 1995 and standing here in the rain and cold, it's hard to believe that spring will ever come again.

We will not forget watching this community of professionals come together—housekeepers and doctors, nursing staff, technicians, administrators, secretaries, transporters, supply clerks, therapists, chaplains, and hundreds of others working side by side. We will not forget the sounds of chaos, tempered by a sense of order and assurance that comes from doing a job and doing it well. We will not forget the feeling of unity as together we shared our skills and knowledge, sorrow and compassion. We will not forget, and we can only hope that someday Spring will come again.

And today, as we dedicate these two trees, one in memory of those who were killed or injured, their families and friends, and one in honor of our University Hospitals that joined hands to preserve life and offer comfort. And as we plant them side by side with branches touching and roots intertwining, we will not forget how our lives touch, affect, and are affected by others. We will not forget those with whom we work, help give meaning to our lives.

So this time next year, when we see blossoms covering these trees and we notice that they are a little taller, a little fuller and a little stronger and we hear birds chattering and singing as they rest in the branches, our certainty that we will never forget shall be accomplished by the realization that indeed, Spring has come again."

The following two submissions come from a very grand Lady in Houston, Texas, Susan Smeltzer. In 1976, Susan received the Distinguished Alumni Award from the University of Oklahoma City for "The Bald Eagle March," which she composed, a copy of which is now housed in the Jimmy Carter Presidential Library in Atlanta, Georgia

THE BALD EAGLE MARCH

BY

SUSAN SMELTZER

*Thee I honor
For thee I hold all trust and hope within
with freedom to protect me
from iniquity*

*For thee I give my strength
and seek for understanding mind
to shape, to mold, to show one
where the roads within thee lie*

*Thee I serve
For thee I sacrifice myself
and pledge anew my faith
to maintain it for thy will*

*In thee I search for the truth
and pray for fresh new insight
into the instability and unrest
that plagues thee from the fall
of all mankind*

*Thee I love
For thee I pride myself with thoughts to hold
and cherish the symbols and beauties of our land*

*To thee I look once again and there the
Great Bald Eagle stands
Rejoice I now in proclamation
America thee be mine*

I KNOW YOU HEARD THE BUGLE CALL

BY

SUSAN SMELTZER

*All was completely silent now as the great tragedy was learned,
and my insides cried out for all of them.*

*Soon the world would stop and point toward the scene...
it was in Oklahoma City that was in a frozen shock of anguish,
that penetrated above the cries and unrest there,
that day of horror on April 19, 1995.*

*As I looked upward in despair,
I thought I heard the bugle cry out,
to say farewell to those dear ones who died there...
for the bugle has played before...
for those brave ones too, who died in battle.*

*But some found the miracle of life still there
while many dear ones were transcended
into the Golden pathway that was bathed with tears,
because we were still here.*

*How strange it is what we learn together
in these precious moments of existence
as time passes by.*

*We laugh together, we cry together,
and those innocent ones there...
they died together as the sick animal raged in those walls.*

(Cont. on pg 108)

I KNOW YOU HEARD THE BUGLE CALL (Cont.)

*It was the bugle call that seemed to sing a silent prayer
for those in that shattered shell...
it seemed to soothe the hurt and it called to those
whose season had ended
that left us with their precious memories in our time.*

*It touched all of them for different reasons
and called out for peace and comfort within a time,
and within a season...
I know you heard it.*

*The golden call must have been an Angel
that carried many over to a new dawn.*

*The bugle call will always be there for them,
perhaps to be carried in the wind,
or in the stillness that strangely meets all
who see that place of glory for all of them.*

*And we'll live it in our thoughts,
and in our hearts, and in our dreams
of them in our time, and we'll listen
as the bugle call goes on.*

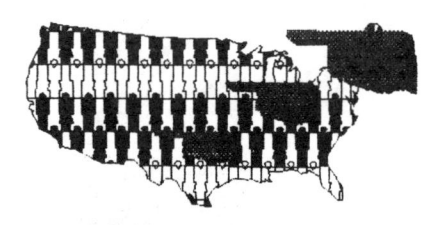

AMERICA REUNITED

BY

STEVIE FARRAND

Through a crisp and perfect blue true morning's dream,
a spring was scattered,
dreams were shattered,
by a blast that bludgeoned
innocence and guileless schemes,
tore at our heart and ripped its seams.

And America the Beautiful became America the terrible
in one premeditated and unbearable
act against itself.

And when the twilight settled
on broken concrete and twisted metal,
over glimmering hope and fathomless pain,
the Angels in denim and khaki remained,
tireless in working, in rescue, in searching...
Knights clad in honor in an Oklahoma rain.

Helping hands across all the land,
reached back with to fill
our torn and shattered space,
wore ribbons of blue and prayed...
for each unaccountable face.

So now, the vigil is over
and the last child has gone home,
with love unending, we begin our mending,
and the healing has begun.
Dreams that were dreamt, can be dreamt again,
our tears are joy, mixed with pain,
and for all the hideous thing that was done,
a greater love, remains...
The love extended has requited
and we are once again, America Reunited!!

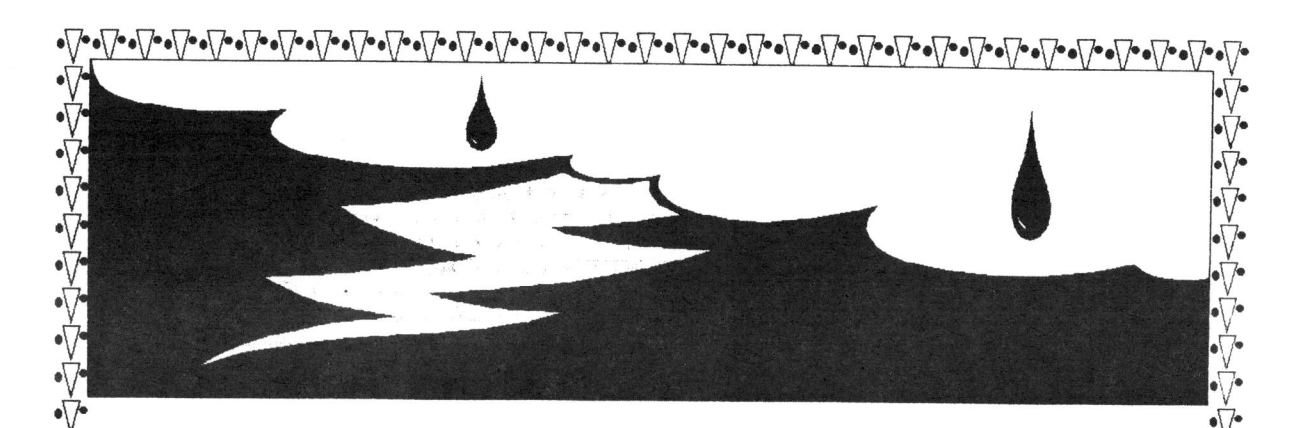

THE BATTLE ZONE

BY

PHIL BLACK

In the smoke, a baby's cry breaks the silence,
the dead are fortunate.
Most watch in a desperate helplessness
while others speed to do what they can.
Quickly people transcend their despair into hate
and curse those who are responsible,
others curse God.

Unnoticed, a wounded pigeon limps
to the curb and dies.
Bodies drape the concrete as the sky darkens
with the coming storm.

Still later, the flashing halogens
from emergency vehicles lend an illusion
of carnival at the onset of darkness.

A nation watches and embraces their loved ones
and we mourn...again.
Thunder rumbles across this Battle Zone
as the sky breaks into tears.

OKLAHOMA CITY TRAGEDY

BY

ROSETTA E. ROSS

*Death is something we all have to face.
But when taken by tragedy it's such a disgrace.*

*We must all pull together to help one and all,
and let not the bad and evil drag us down to fall.*

*We'll never forget the victims of the Oklahoma City bomb,
but we must all be strong and try to stay calm.*

*We'll pray and remember to help those who survived,
and we'll ask God to lead us and be our guide.*

*The children are the great loss in Oklahoma City.
It's so sad and heartless and such a great pity.*

*As I am a mother, I can only imagine the pain,
to lose a dear child, I think it's insane.*

*"Why?" is the question we all have to ask
did this terrible tragedy happen will it ever come to pass?*

*Much thanks to the rescuers, helpers and volunteers,
our heartfelt "Thank You" through our love, hugs and tears.*

*To all the families and survivors with love,
May God be with you and shed light from above.*

TO MY CHILDREN
FAITH, JUSTIN
AND SHAILA

BY

JAMES C. YEAROUT

I wasn't there for all your life-though I might have been...
but what time I had with you, realize that
I have loved you through it all-the rough times, the good times.
We look back and see that God was forming us
and growing us to be his best.
Each of you has made my life more complete and I
pray God is not finished with me yet,
but will give us more time together.
Love is our strongest bond,
forming beyond compare-and the love of a Father,
like a Mother's, is always there.
I hope that I gave you through the years we had together,
a part of myself that will help you through
the stormy weather.
You are all an important part of my life...
I love you with all my heart and give thanks
each day that God gave you to me!

Editors Note: The contributor of this poem is a very dear friend of mine. He is the Commander of Metropolitan Oklahoma City Chapter 568, Military Order of the Purple Heart of which I am also the Adjutant. Jim said he really didn't know what to say about those who had perished so he wrote this to his children who were fortunate enough to not have been associated with the bombing.

MEMORY OF THOSE WE LOVED

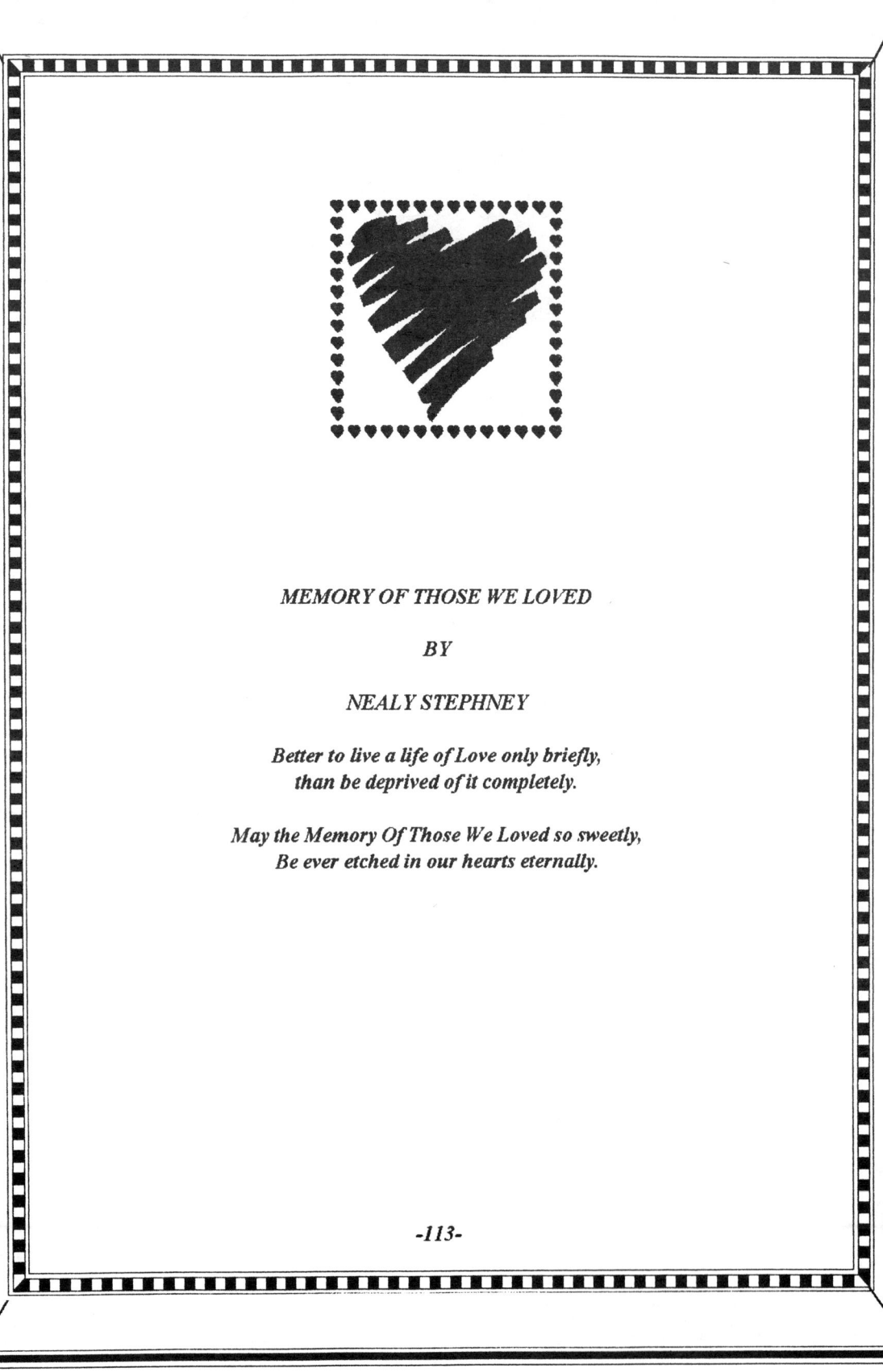

BY

NEALY STEPHNEY

*Better to live a life of Love only briefly,
than be deprived of it completely.*

*May the Memory Of Those We Loved so sweetly,
Be ever etched in our hearts eternally.*

MY BLANKET

BY

BETH ODLE

My blanket will be a cover of wildflowers
if I should die in the Spring,
when all things begin to grow
and the birds begin to sing.

My blanket will be the green green grass
if I should die in the summers heat
when the roses bloom
and the hive is full of honey sweet.

My blanket will be leaves of red and gold
if I should die in the fall when all things wither
and the birds fly South
to answer Nature's call.

My blanket will be the pure white snow,
if I should die in the winter's cold,
when the earth falls asleep,
and everything grows old.

But no matter what the season,
and my body is placed neath' the sod,
my soul shall ever live
wrapped in the sweet arms of God!!

OKLAHOMA CITY HEARTLAND

BY

SANDRA ROBINS

On Wednesday morning the world would see,
how the Heartland of America would come to be,
a tragic, gruesome and broken place,
with terror and shock upon our face.
We came together and worked as one,
from coast to coast and sun to sun.
We wait, we listen, we pray to hear,
a cry for help from someone dear.
And then the word comes that we all dread:
"I regret to inform you, your child is dead."
This tears at our heart and makes us ask why,
these innocent people were slated to die.
The world waits and watches in true disbelief,
as the stories are told in the eyes of our grief.
We pray in our hearts and hope it's today
the terrorists are caught with strict prices to pay.
And that's how on Wednesday the whole world would see
how the Heartland of America would come to be.

This poem came all the way from Nova Scotia, showing that all the world mourns for Oklahoma and those that lost so much

THE ANGELS OF OKLAHOMA

BY

PAULA MARIE McISAAC

*Dear God above, the news is out,
the tragedy the whole world is talking about,
the children, men and women who lost their lives,
the brothers sisters, husbands and wives.*

*They mourn as we all do
that so many lives are gone because of so few.
I look at my children because of this mess
and I make each day for them the very best.*

*As we all take for granted
our towns are safe and sound,
when in just one moment
our children are nowhere to be found.*

*I know all hearts in Canada
are with everyone there.
There are still a lot of
people in this world who really care.*

*As I watch TV and listen
to your stories and fears
I find it hard to control
my feelings and tears.*

*I wish I could be there to comfort someone,
but since I cannot I'm sending my love
to all the Angels of Oklahoma
who now protect us from above!*

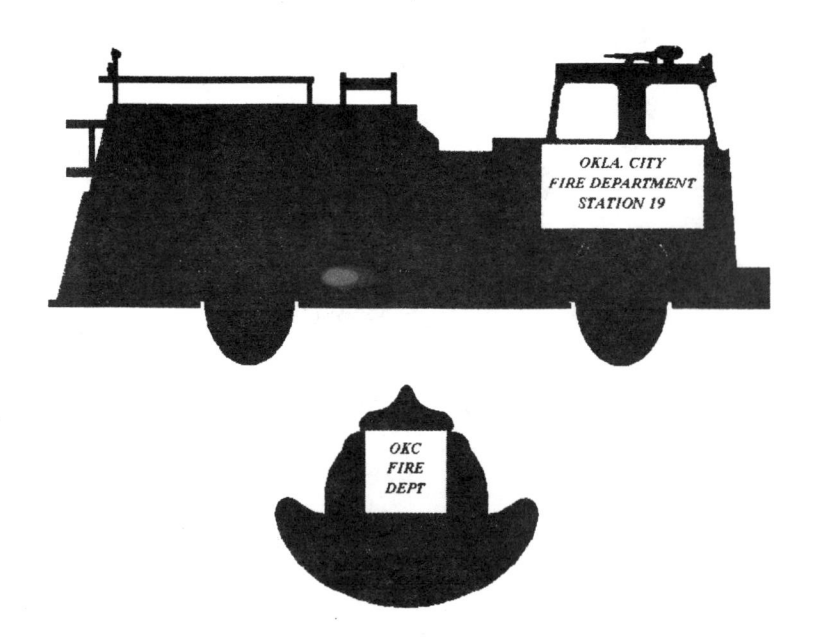

OUR FIREMEN

BY

KIMBERLY CHEW

*They have a gift from above,
to do the job they all love.*

*They sit at the station to listen and wait,
for all our lives are in their fate.*

*It's not all fun and games in their life,
if you don't believe that,
just ask a fireman's wife!!*

*It shouldn't take much to see,
what a fireman can do for you and me.*

Editors Note: Mrs. Chews husband is a fireman who assisted in the recovery and rescue operations

WE SHALL NEVER FORGET

The day started out as the best of times for the citizens of Oklahoma City. It soon turned out to be the worst of times. Someone declared a war of hatred upon our city. The sound of the bomb was heard eighty miles away and the smoke blackened the horizon signalling chaos, death and mutilation. Our children, parents, grandparents, aunts, uncles, nieces, nephews and cousins were made sacrificial lambs to appease a twisted sense of justice. We mourn our great losses now and into the future, however, God in his mercy and wisdom sent to us many, many noble men, women and children from across the world to share in our grief and help us cope in the aftermath of this dastardly and horrific deed—Anna Slaughter

A CHILD SPEAKS

BY ANNA SLAUGHTER

Why do you hate me so? I am an innocent child.
Come, take me in your arms,
hold me, cuddle me awhile.

Don't turn your face from me, am I so hard to touch?
Or will my tenderness soften you?
Are you afraid to love too much?

My hands reach out to you to help me be my best.
Give me your hands in return
and I will stand the test.

You reached out to me, not close but afar,
how you touched me and went away.
You left me not as I once was,
but hurt, bleeding, with joy at bay.

But I have risen above you, you will never touch me again.
I am soaring high above in the clouds
where love and cuddling ever remain!!

GOD'S WONDERFUL WORK

*BY
CHUCK NORRIS
(EDITOR)*

*April's windy grace,
the smile on a small child's face.
The bark of a dog which touched his heart,
this is truly a part of
God's Wonderful Work.*

*The rushing sounds of a blue waterfall,
the bouncing of a little rubber ball,
the twitting of a little bird,
which can by a child be heard.
This is truly a part of
God's Wonderful Work.*

*The trees with their leaves of brown,
the patter of little feet on the path to town,
the laughter of a little child as
he runs and plays,
that brings cheer to his Mother's day.
This is truly a part of
God's Wonderful Work.*

Editors Note: This was the first poem I wrote as a child. I wrote it one day when my dearly beloved Mother was writing poetry and she said I should write one to show God that I loved him. I was in the seventh grade.

A COMMON BOND

BY

KELLIE SADLER

WEDNESDAY AFTERNOON:

We sit,
a group of strangers unwillingly drawn together.
Blank stares, silent weeping, unflinching hope,
groups transfixed to television sets,
waiting for news, volunteers eager to help.
Evening approaches, the sun sets.
No word.
We sit.

THURSDAY DAWNS:

Bright, clear, crisp. Was it all a dream?
Some faces, familiar but not known.
More tears today as reality becomes clearer.
The numbness wearing off.
Food, friends, supplies arrive in steady streams.
Constant motion, constant noise.
Blank faces waiting.
We sit.

(Cont. on pg 121)

A COMMON BOND (Cont.)

FRIDAY:

Sunny, calm. Same faces, though not so many now,
as silent groups leave with their news.
Hope still alive, nervous laughter, television always on.
Tears, frustration, anger, still waiting,
We sit.

SATURDAY NOW:

Cold, windy, raining.
Not much searching today.
Count raise, more names released, hope still lives.
For most, no news, so still,
We sit.

SUNDAY:

Anticipation, surely today, we'll know.
Visiting dignataries, a president, a reverend,
an Attorney General.
Choir voices, both old and young,
Teddy bears and tears.
Back to the church, no news today.
Still waiting,
We sit.

MONDAY:

Has it been six days?
We still sit, waiting for our news.
Generosity continues to pour in.
Flowers from around the world.
Cards and prayers from children everywhere.
Five-thirty, we finally know.
No more sitting, our wait is over.

IN LOVING MEMORY OF FRANKIE ANN MERRELL

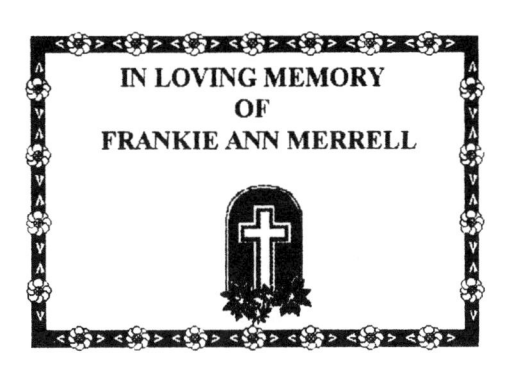

I CAN SEE HER NOW

BY

DONNA SAWATZKY

High top white walkers, sneakers, high heels,
tricycle, bicycle, then four wheels.
Sweet toothless smiles filled with dimples,
tiny hands, gangly arms, legs and pimples.
Sunsuits, denim, satin and pearls,
baby fuzz, dog ears, braids and curls.
Sand box dolls, and Mickey Mouse,
toy stove, fridge, her very first house.
Newborn cries and a two year old's squalls,
teenage phone calls and shopping malls.
A baby girl, young woman and loving mother,
a beautiful person who is like no other.

She's the only one, she is a Daughter!!

IN ANGEL'S ARMS

BY

MARGARET MARTIN

In Angel's Arms is where the children are.
In Angel's Arms they are taken up.
In Angel's Arms they are comforted and safe.
In Angel's Arms their little hurts are all gone.
In Angel's Arms their place is in the hands of Jesus
to live and play, happily, forever more.
In Angel's Arms is where the parents will be
when God calls them home,
and unites them together in His Family.

A NATION'S PRAYER

BY

AMY PARRISH

*Dear Lord, be with the victims
who have met you up above,
and Lord, be with their loved ones,
give them strength and love.*

*Wrap your arms around the children, Lord,
erase all their fears.
Give them families to love them,
and to wipe away their tears.*

*Guide the rescue workers, Lord,
as they face the toughest days,
let their bravery be a beacon,
in our nation's darkest hour.*

*And Lord, be with the country
that has seen such tragic pain,
we are all overcoming this tragedy
and good will rise again!*

OKLAHOMA CITY—1995

BY

ROBERTA W. NORRIS

All of our lives we've been told,
life can be over in the twinkling of an eye.
Yet we take it for granted
we'll see our loved ones again,
when in the morning we tell them, "Good-bye."
So who would have thought
that on this beautiful spring morning
in the middle of America's Heartland,
so many lives would be snuffed out early
by such a cruel act from another American's hand.
They say they did it for revenge,
at the government they were mad,
but why did they have to take the lives
of innocent children, grandparents, moms and dads?
We may not remember all the folks who moved
pieces of granite and steel,
or maneuvered the cranes to get people out alive.
But the world will never forget the disastrous bombing
of the Federal Building in Oklahoma City
That morning in April of 1995!

..Dedicated to the victims of the disaster and all those
who gave so very much of themselves
in order that others might live..
Roberta Norris

God is Love

TO OUR HORROR

BY

T. J. McCLOUD

*To our horror, the flash, the sounds, the screams
in our dreams, the hurt, the dead, the heroes
now Angels. Angels.
They walk through our nightmares,
our own brothers- -killed
our children who were so unaware.*

*So impartial to the motives of hate,
yet with that one push of a button,
with that one twist of a dial, with that one light of a fuse,
our children's innocence and youth has been denied,
so we now ask, "What shall we do?"*

*What with the lost and buried in the black abyss,
what with the building torn and bruised?
What with the tears of the family and friends,
of the fellow countrymen?*

*On our own we are helpless,
on our own we are gone,
on our own we will be left in ruins,
but with Love,
we conquer all!*

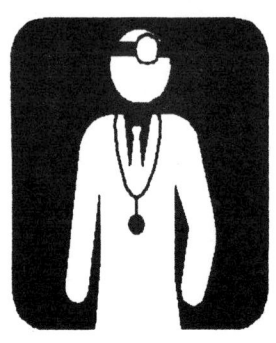

FOR WHATEVER REASON

BY

DEBORAH ELAINE COLE

*For whatever reason it doesn't matter,
many lives have been shattered.
The lives of the children that we cherish,
for whatever reason, had to perish.*

*All differences now set aside,
we all work together, side by side.
Like the old saying, as you can see,
now is the time for all good men
to come to the aid of their country.*

*The Oklahoma City population has doubled,
as people came together to aid a city in trouble.
Nothing we can do or say,
can take the pain away.*

*We all joined hands in troubled times,
to piece together the puzzle
of a horrendous crime.
All other life has been put on hold,
as we gather to hear the news unfold.*

*All the nurses and doctors from afar,
will never be able to repair the scars.
We can only pray that pain will ease with time,
and remember always,
there is no punishment to fit this crime!*

SPECIAL DEDICATIONS
FOR
SOME SPECIAL PEOPLE

MOM AND DAD

*I WOULDN'T BE HERE TODAY IF IT WASN'T FOR YOU,
YOU'VE ALWAYS BEEN BEHIND ME IN EVERYTHING I DO.
YOU'VE GIVEN ME HOPE WHEN I THOUGHT NONE WAS LEFT.*

*YOU'VE BEEN NOTHING BUT THE BEST.
DAD, YOU HELPED TEACH ME WRONG FROM RIGHT,
AND YOU NEVER LET ME GET FAR FROM SIGHT.
MOM, YOU TAUGHT ME HOW TO PRAY,
YOU ARE THE LIGHT OF EACH DAY.*

*THEN EARLY ONE MORN,
MY SON WAS BORN.
AND I BEGAN TO SEE,
THE LOVE YOU HAD FOR ME.
YOU TOOK US IN WHEN TIMES GOT TOUGH,
YOU ALWAYS SAID ALL THE RIGHT STUFF.
THEN GOD SENT TOM TO ME,
AND MADE MY LIFE COMPLETE,
AND NOTHING IS MORE IMPORTANT TO
ME THAN MY FAMILY....DEBORAH COLE*

A WORD OF THANKS

CHUCK, THANKS FOR ALL THE LONG HOURS YOU PUT IN TYPING PRECIOUS MEMORIES, AND THANKS FOR TYPING AND RE-TYPING POEMS TO FINALLY GET A FINISHED PRODUCT THAT SATISFIED US ALL...

WE COULDN'T HAVE DONE IT WITHOUT YOU!!!
DANIEL TOM DEMOSS

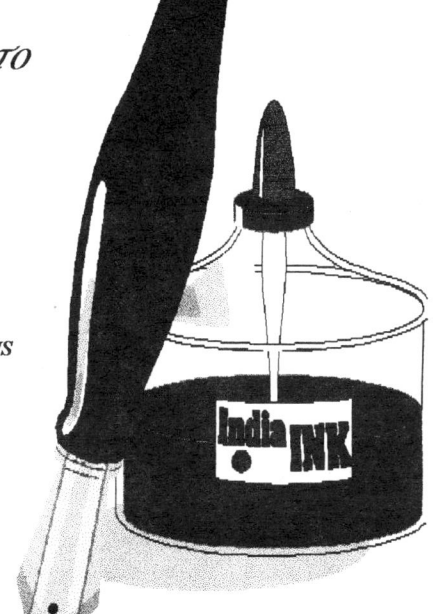

Heartworks Publishing Co.
P.O. Box 94386
Oklahoma City, OK 73143

Volume discounts available
Send SASE for information.
Allow 4 to 6 weeks for shipping.
All orders must be prepaid.

ORDER FORM

Please send me_____ copy (s) of *Precious Memories*
@ $10.95 each.

Please send me_____ *Precious Memories T-Shirts (T-Shirts have same imprint as*
@ $11.95 each   *cover of book)*

Subtotal $_____

Postage & Handling $ 3.50 Per Copy
Oklahoma residents add local & state sales tax $_____

TOTAL$_____

SHIP TO:

Name_____
        Please type or print legibly
Address_____

City/State/Zip_____

Phone: Area Code & Number_____

PAYMENT METHOD:

Money Order or Cashiers Check only. (No postal money orders) Please do not send cash

I have enclosed a Money Order/Cashiers Check made payable to
Heartworks Publishing Co. in the amount of $_____

Please charge my order to: **VISA Card #**_____
                                    Expiration Date:_____

                    Mastercard#_____
                                    Expiration Date:_____

Signature:_____

Send order and payment to:
Heartworks Publishing Co.
P.O. Box 94386
Oklahoma City, OK 73143